Testimonials

In life there are people that you meet that leave you with a smile, feeling good and with renewed enthusiasm. Glenn Flood is one of those people. His culinary experience is long and varied and can't be questioned – but it's his love of food and hospitality that sets him apart. In industry circles he's a stalwart – a passionate and creative chef, trainer, educator, mentor and an advocate for doing business better. Glenn's book will help you shift your thinking and take your hospitality career to the next level.

Gary Mehigan
Chef, Restaurateur, Author, TV presenter

I have seen Glenn operate in a senior leadership capacity for fifteen years, and I can confidently say he is the most inspiring colleague I have had the privilege of working alongside. Beyond professional expertise, he has become a trusted adviser, business mentor, and close friend. Glenn is a true leader who brings an infectious energy to every collaboration. His ability to drive projects with precision, innovation, and excellence is unmatched. Whether in hospitality, marketing, operations or business consultancy, Glenn's impact is transformative. I'm excited to see how this book will continue to build on his legacy of inspiring clients to be better in business and life.

Samuel Burke
Business Development Manager, Corporate Chef
Meat & Livestock Australia

From an apprentice to Executive Chef – Glenn has always had that special spark. His professionalism and experience in the food industry are first-class, but it's his contagious energy that leaves an impression. His book, Secret Sauce, is like a great recipe – easy to follow, honest and full of flavour. It's the kind of read that makes you want to step up your kitchen leadership game.

Elke Travers
Commercial Development Chef
Nestle Professional

I've worked with Glenn in various roles for over a decade, and it's clear he is more than just an Executive Chef. His passion for innovation, creative flair, and leadership is inspiring. Glenn doesn't just raise the bar – he leads by example, driving results while coaching chefs to become exceptional managers. With 15 venues and 800 staff, I brought Glenn in to reshape, train, and inspire our teams. His training programs have been transformative, helping us grow and strengthen the business. Glenn Flood is the secret sauce. He inspires people to be their best, and in turn, our business thrives.

Russell Evans
Executive Director
Pegasus Leisure Group

Glenn truly embodies the essence of effective leadership. Having known him for over a decade, I've witnessed firsthand his profound grasp of team dynamics and his exceptional ability to guide with clarity and insight. Glenn wears the 'maillot jaune' among kitchen leaders, consistently at the front of the pack due to his remarkable ability to swiftly implement feedback and insights. 'Secret Sauce – The Proven Recipe for Kitchen Leadership' is more than a book; it's a practical manual, crafted from years of genuine experience and dedication to the art of leadership. For those ready to enhance their impact in the culinary world, Glenn's book offers indispensable strategies and wisdom. It's an essential resource for any chef stepping into a managerial role.

Dave Lourdes
Founder, Evolving Human Potential

This great industry has allowed me to connect and meet the most incredible humans. Glenn is that and more. A chef of the highest order. Not only a man in the business of flavour but a man with a modern-day calming mindset. Most of all he is a caring human. If you want to become a better chef then read his book – *now*.

George Calombaris
Chef, Culinary Curator, Dream Weaver

SECRET SAUCE

The Proven Recipe for
Kitchen Leadership

GLENN FLOOD

First published by Ultimate World Publishing 2025
Copyright © 2025 Glenn Flood

ISBN

Paperback: 978-1-923425-77-4
Ebook: 978-1-923425-78-1

Glenn Flood has asserted his rights under the Copyright, Designs and Patents Act 1988 to be identified as the author of this work. The information in this book is based on the author's experiences and opinions. The publisher specifically disclaims responsibility for any adverse consequences which may result from use of the information contained herein. Permission to use information has been sought by the author. Any breaches will be rectified in further editions of the book.

All rights reserved. No part of this publication may be reproduced, stored in or introduced into a retrieval system, or transmitted in any form, or by any means (electronic, mechanical, photocopying, recording or otherwise) without the prior written permission of the author. Any person who does any unauthorised act in relation to this publication may be liable to criminal prosecution and civil claims for damages. Enquiries should be made through the publisher.

Cover design: Ultimate World Publishing
Layout and typesetting: Ultimate World Publishing
Editor: James Salmon
Author photo: Eddy Khayat

Ultimate World Publishing
Diamond Creek,
Victoria Australia 3089
www.writeabook.com.au

Dedication

For Nikita, Ethan and Lucas

Contents

Author's Note	1
Foreword	3
Introduction	5
Your Guide to Secret Sauce	9
Appetiser	11
The First Mastery - People	**15**
1 Milk Crate Sessions	17
2 Can You Handle the Heat?	35
3 Fuelling the Fire	47
The Second Mastery - Finance	**65**
4 Beyond the Menu	67
5 The Ecosystem	81
6 Making Dough	95
The Third Mastery - Safety	**117**
7 Avoiding Burnout	119
8 Mise en Place	135
9 The Heartbeat	147

The Fourth Mastery - Quality	**163**
10 Umami	165
11 Every Plate, Every Time	179
12 Hone the Knife	195
Afterword	207
About the Author	209
The Next Steps	213
Bibliography	217

Author's Note

I'm so grateful that you're holding this book in your hands. My hope is that it contains at least one idea that sparks something big for you – an idea that changes your trajectory as a leader and sets you on a new pathway to success. Even the smallest ripple can gather momentum, creating transformative results in how you motivate your team, enhance the customer journey, amplify your creativity or impact kitchen culture.

The truth is leaders aren't born – they're made.

Secret Sauce – The Proven Recipe for Kitchen Leadership is the culmination of almost three decades of experience working with high performers, business owners, progressive CEOs, executives, general managers, team leaders and chefs of all levels. The concepts, methods, and strategies in this book are ones I've been refining, implementing and teaching in kitchens, masterclasses and boardrooms.

But this book isn't just about tips and tools – it's about building the mindset you need to lead with authenticity and with purpose. I've poured my heart into making this a practical and relatable guide, one that I hope will inspire you to embrace leadership as both a skill and a journey.

To everyone who has been part of this journey with me – my mentors, peers, colleagues, friends and the incredible leaders I've had the privilege to work with – thank you. Your trust, wisdom and openness have guided my career.

To my boys, Ethan and Lucas – thank you for your encouragement, love, and patience as I've dedicated countless hours to honing my craft. To Nikita, my soul mate, best friend and wife – thank you for the morning walks, listening to my musings, unwavering support and keeping me in check on this roller coaster of life. I am so grateful for everything you do for our tribe.

A special shoutout to those inspiring conversations that have left a lasting impression on my career. Mum and Dad for the possibility and positivity, Paul's persistence, milk crate sessions with Tobes, coaching conversations with Dave, Harvey's hustle, Sammy's motivation, Mario's curiosity and Russell's operational rhythm. You may not have realised it at the time, but your words stuck with me and helped shape the ideas in this book.

And lastly to you, the reader – thank you for taking the time to invest in your development. I'm deeply grateful for your trust in these pages, and I can't wait to see where this journey takes you! Here's to unlocking your potential and creating your own secret sauce.

Foreword

Leadership in the kitchen is a real art — it's not just about being great at cooking. It's about inspiring your team, staying calm under pressure and making the people around you better. Over the years, I've met many talented chefs and the ones who stand out are the ones who know how to lead with heart. Glenn Flood is one of those people.

From the first meeting, I could see he wasn't just about the food — he was about the people. He's the kind of leader who lifts everyone up, whether they're just starting out or already at the top of their game. He's got this amazing ability to see potential in others and help them unlock it.

In *Secret Sauce — The Proven Recipe for Kitchen Leadership*, Glenn shares everything he's learned about what it really takes to lead in the high-stakes world of professional kitchens. It's not just practical advice (though there's loads of that); it's also packed with stories, insights and life lessons that anyone can learn from. This book isn't just for chefs — it's for anyone who wants to lead with purpose and bring out the best in their team.

What I love about Glenn's approach is how down-to-earth and honest it is. He doesn't sugarcoat the challenges of leadership, but he also makes it clear that the hard work is worth it. It's not about being perfect – it's about being real, building trust, and creating a space where people feel valued and inspired to do their best.

I'm pumped that Glenn has written this book. It's a game-changer for anyone who reads it. So, dive in and get ready to discover the 'Secret Sauce' that makes a truly great kitchen leader.

Here's to leading with heart and making a difference, one kitchen at a time.

Tobie Puttock

Introduction

Why This Book?

Georges August Escoffier was known as the King of Chefs and the Chef of Kings. He famously consolidated and systemised the organisation of the brigade de cuisine – a hierarchical system inspired by his experiences in the military that brought order and efficiency to the kitchen.

This was designed to create consistency from chaos. Workflow, mise en place, recipes, procedures, habits, discipline, communication and systems. All this to allow a brigade of chefs to have a consistent output of food.

The structure created opportunity for young chefs to start at the bottom, learn the basics, move onto the next section and progress with the learning until reaching the status of Chef de Cuisine, or Executive Chef. Escoffier's legacy and influence remains in kitchens around the world to this day.

I came through a traditional 4-year chef's apprenticeship. I'd worked in cafés, restaurants, clubs and hotels during my training years – a young chef with a thirst for knowledge and an appetite to travel (and snowboard).

This was the time to make mistakes, fuck things up, go under during service, work with experienced chefs and learn the foundations of the craft. It was a time of split shifts, transient labour, unregulated award wages, cash payments, high staff turnover and high pressure. Repetition led to consistency. Consistency led to muscle memory. Muscle memory embedded habits. This was the traditional way of learning.

Enter the era of disruption.

In today's climate, the access to knowledge, engagement with food, ability to influence and appetite to scroll obscene amounts of online content has never been greater. Why would anyone take years to learn a craft, when they can download a tutorial on their smartphone and simply have a crack at it?

Why simmer a master stock for 20 years, adding a supreme level of depth and complexity when you can do a 5-minute 'hack' or cheat version and still have a half-decent product?

The world has shifted. Food media has evolved. MasterChef Australia captured the global imagination of viewers in over 160 countries and spawned a whole new generation of home cooks and foodies who were exposed to previously unknown industry legends, all only too happy to share their craft to propel the hospitality industry forward.

Why This Book?

Consumers are more educated. Celebrity chefs are on the rise. Everyone has an emotional opinion about food. Cooking shows have their own dedicated channels and there are opportunities in the food industry that did not even exist several years ago. Having two former MasterChef contestants now come full circle and become judges on the show that trained them is testament to the fact that the formula has merit.

These are unprecedented and exciting times to be a chef! Opportunity is everywhere.

In the food service industry, employers are screaming for skilled staff, retention is one of the biggest challenges and chef apprenticeships are declining. It's the perfect storm.

I have witnessed (on far too many occasions) an inexperienced young chef suddenly elevated to head chef status, simply because they are the last person standing and the employer is desperate. This is fraught with danger. They take the leap from still learning their craft to suddenly being accountable for managing a team and controlling a multi-million dollar food operation.

I often hear comments from owners and managers like:

'I have no experience running a kitchen, I just leave them to it.'
'I pay them like a head chef so they just need to work it out.'
'Chef needs to get the team under control.'
'Chef is in a bad mood today – stay out of the way.'
'Chefs are a pain in the ass.'

Circumstances like this are a real opportunity for the upcoming chef to:

- Increase their remuneration
- Build their 'brand'
- Put into practice the habits they have acquired
- Put their stamp on the menu
- Work more closely with the suppliers
- Cut their teeth in a leadership role

The challenges they are facing include:

- Gaining the respect of the team
- Controlling labour
- Meeting financial targets
- Keeping their ego in check
- Managing expectations
- Communicating effectively
- Being overworked
- Not knowing what they don't know
- Frustration and burnout

When chefs reach this stage in their career, cooking is the easiest thing they will do in their day. Yet it is no longer the focus. The skills that got them to this point are not the skills that will take them forward. It's the constant noise of other 'non-cooking' activities that come with the role that most chefs are not trained to perform and ill-equipped to perfect.

They need a blueprint, a formula……a *Secret Sauce*.

Your Guide to Secret Sauce

"The mind that opens to a new idea never returns to its original size."
                              - Albert Einstein

A book is a conversation with the author... and the right conversation at the right time has the power to transform your trajectory.

I appreciate you are a busy person, so wanted to share my thoughts on how to get the most out of this book. You don't need to read it cover to cover…. Consider these chapters the ingredients you need to be a kickass kitchen leader. How they are best blended together will be different for everyone.

I've distilled the messages into bite-sized pieces – so if you've read a concept or idea that resonates, consider how you can act on it and get results. That might be enough reading for the day. I encourage you to think of this as a reference guide

Secret Sauce

to jump in and out of, depending on the challenge you are faced with. This provides the best leverage of your time.

When I run masterclasses, I always advise the participants to sample the dish then follow the recipe the way it was initially intended. Like all good recipes, there are different ways to assemble them, depending on your level of experience.

Consider these chapters the main ingredients. Read, learn, form opinions, adjust the seasoning and build on them. Once you feel confident, rework and adapt the recipe to make it your own.

And if you make it better – please share it back with me! I'd love to know your additions.

By the end of this book my goal for you is to walk away with the confidence, the insight, the ability and the tools to lead your kitchen team to success. What I love about working with chefs is they are task-oriented and driven. All the theory in the world means nothing without putting steps in place and making shit happen.

My role is to be your mentor, to share stories, provide insights and level up your kitchen leadership. There's a lot of work to be done but I know that if you've read this far, you're up for the challenge. It's time to fire up the burners!

Appetiser

Kitchen Leadership

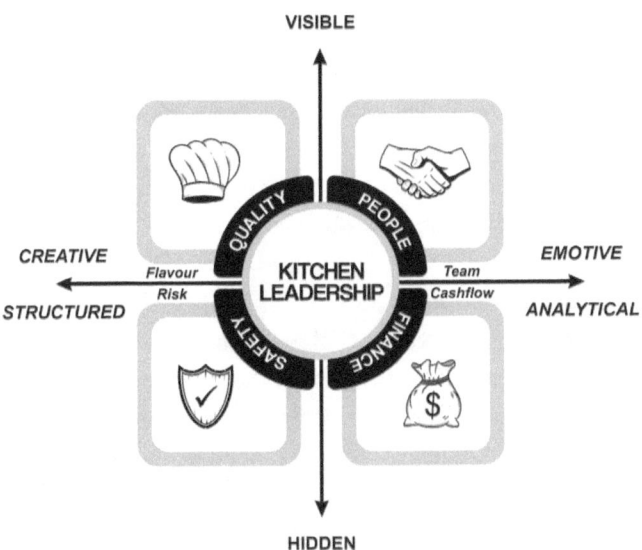

I have invested many years analysing the core elements of kitchen leadership. This has led to the conclusion that the expectations of a kitchen leader can be classified under four pillars:

People. Finance. Safety. Quality.

These are the pillars that underpin all the content, stories and lessons contained within Secret Sauce. I've worked with hundreds of chefs over the last three decades and found that most head chefs have elements of these masteries – but finding them all in balance is rare.

You might be a fantastic technician on the plate, but struggle with how to read a profit and loss sheet. You could be the kind of chef that is amazing with food safety and compliance yet struggle to craft a menu under time pressure. You might find that you really just love to cook and work with amazing produce (because it doesn't talk back) but absolutely cringe at the idea of running a kitchen meeting – where everyone's watching and hanging on your every word.

Mastery 1 - People
Your brigade is the heartbeat of the kitchen. It doesn't matter if you're the fastest on the pans or the strongest on the grill – you win and lose as a team. When engagement is high, you build trust, loyalty, and a crew that shows up under pressure. That energy flows into every service – lifting standards, driving teamwork and maintaining consistency. Strong teams don't just deliver great food – they develop a great culture.

Mastery 2 - Finance
Sustainable success in the kitchen goes far beyond managing wastage or negotiating good deals. If you're in it for the long game, you need to understand cashflow and know how to turn a profit from every plate. Whether you're already running your own business or dreaming of it down the track, food is a high-stakes game – and your menu is your number one sales tool. You don't need to be an accountant, but boosting your financial literacy will elevate your leadership and help you make smarter, sharper decisions.

Mastery 3 - Safety
Safety and compliance might not be the sexiest topic in the kitchen, but it's non-negotiable. It's not just a checklist – it's a culture, a habit, a standard that should be second nature, not an afterthought. The kitchen is a high-risk workplace – for your team, your customers, and your brand. It's physically demanding, high-pressure, and filled with equipment that can cause real harm if not handled with care. Embedding safe systems and habits isn't optional – it's a core part of your kitchen leadership journey.

Mastery 4 - Quality
Quality is the seasoning in your secret sauce – the bold, unmistakable flavour that keeps people coming back. It's the relentless pursuit of excellence, pushing creativity, and transforming a good dish into an unforgettable experience. It's all about consistency, finesse, and precision in execution. This is where your skills shine – like an alchemist blending elements to create something extraordinary. Quality is your umami booster. It's what sets you apart – the difference that makes a difference.

The First Mastery

People

Chapter 1

Milk Crate Sessions

Engagement

"You can learn a lot about someone when you share a meal together."
- Anthony Bourdain

You know the drill. You've been there before. You've seen it hundreds of times just outside the back door of the kitchen, in an alley way or loading dock. A few chefs, sitting on milk crates, hanging out and talking shit. Whether it be a short rest, quick smoko or taking in the 'fresh' air just before service, milk crate sessions should never be underrated. From Melbourne to Morrocco, Sydney to Singapore. It's part of the culture.

Secret Sauce

This chapter is about team engagement and communication skills. While your cooking expertise got you to this senior level in the brigade – it is not going to get you to the next level. Engaging your team and leveraging their skill is what you need to focus on. In this chapter you're going to learn the art of impacting those around you and inspiring them to perform, because at the end of the day a team is only as strong as their weakest link.

As a chef stepping up into leadership – it's about how you connect with, inspire and get the best out of your team. Everyday moments like short breaks, staff meals, or pre-service meetings become powerful opportunities to communicate with purpose and lead with intent.

You'll dive into practical ways to refine how you talk to your crew, build trust and create a team that performs under pressure. Whether it's learning to balance coaching and mentoring, understanding the value of contact time, or figuring out how your leadership style impacts the brigade, this chapter has you covered.

Get this right, and not only will your kitchen culture thrive, but you'll also save yourself from burnout while taking your career to the next level.

Habits and Rhythm

All kitchen teams have an operational rhythm. It might be a structured pre-start meeting covering customer feedback, production targets and safety or an informal gathering around the coffee machine while sipping that first espresso of the day.

Identifying a habit or 'ritual' that is already ingrained in the fabric of the kitchen and bringing a clear intent into the sessions will focus the team. Planning the message you need to share and how you are going to deliver it will amplify your influence as a leader.

A milk crate session is the perfect opportunity to do this. There is the right amount of informality, energy and comradery flowing to gauge how everyone is feeling, provide quality feedback and share your own thoughts on the service just completed. Instant feedback prevents anyone going home unclear on their performance and contribution to the team.

If someone's section went under, that's OK, we've all been there. What was the tipping point? What did they learn? What support do they need? What will they do to improve? These are great questions to ask.

So why is communication important for you as an emerging kitchen leader?

What tends to happen in the workplace is that your head chef will come to a stage when the role, environment or circumstance is no longer aligned with their interest and they decide to move on. This can happen for any number of reasons, including:

- Burnout
- Pressure
- Timing
- Conflict

- Change of conditions
- Personal circumstances
- Change of direction
- Career progression
- Choice

Sometimes this is planned, and a handover is in place to ensure a smooth transition and minimise any angst among the team. You've most likely experienced this – farewell drinks, acknowledgement of tenure, which creates an opportunity for new leadership. This is best practice. In some cases though, the head chef's departure is swift – with little or no reason provided to the team. When this occurs, someone is needed to step up, fill the gap and make shit happen.

That is why this book exists – to prep you for the challenges ahead.

At the time of taking your first leadership role, all of the habits (good and bad) that you have accumulated over your cooking journey come into play. Before you had a buffer – now there is nowhere to hide. It can be daunting. What tends to happen in this circumstance is that most chefs feel an element of 'imposter syndrome' and try to prove their worth by being the hardest worker in the room. You might hear yourself saying – "Don't worry about it – I'll do it myself".

The benchmark of your skill set as a professional chef is the standard of food being served when you are having a (well-deserved) day off. This is why kitchen habits are so important.

They are the 1%'s that all add up to get the job done in a consistent way. In the same breath, the measure of your overall hygiene standards come down to your casual kitchen hand, their understanding of their responsibilities and their ability to take action. Because that is the potential weakest link and where the risk for your kitchen lies.

Communication
The first step to increasing your engagement levels with those around you is to understand how you're communicating.

- Are you coming across like a dictator and is that working for you?
- Are you reacting to what others are saying or guiding the conversation?
- Are your responses measured or emotionally charged?
- Do you assume your team understands every instruction you give the first time they hear it?
- Are you asking questions and clarifying that your message is landing in the way it was intended?
- Are you framing up the conversation so those you are with understand what you're talking about?

An activity I've run with teams of head chefs is to discuss their thoughts on the leadership styles of two world class British chefs, both of whom I deeply respect – Gordon Ramsay and Jamie Oliver. While the participants may have never met either of them personally, they have formed an opinion from social media, articles, books and television.

Secret Sauce

When asked how they think Gordon Ramsay might lead a kitchen brigade, the descriptions that arise include:

Intense – He demands high energy and focus in the kitchen.
Passionate – His love for food and culinary excellence shines through.
Detail-oriented – He emphasises perfection in every dish and process.
High Standards – He expects nothing but the best from his team.
Disciplined – He enforces strict kitchen protocols and rules.
Inspirational – He motivates his team to push beyond their limits.

As opposed to what their perception might be of Jamie Oliver leading a kitchen brigade, where descriptions include:

Approachable – Warm and easygoing, fostering an inclusive environment.
Innovative – Constantly creating new ideas in the kitchen.
Empathetic – Deeply caring about his team and their personal growth.
Inspirational – Motivates others with his passion for food and community.
Supportive – Encourages his team and offers guidance without micromanaging.
Collaborative – Values teamwork and collective problem-solving.
Nurturing – Invests in the development of young talent, especially disadvantaged youth.

Now these leadership traits are neither right nor wrong – the activity is to demonstrate how humans form perceptions about leaders they may never have met.

Does that mean either of these two chefs are less or more successful than the other? Does this mean that either of these two chefs are not capable of running an efficient kitchen? Does this indicate either chef can't prepare and cook amazing food for their customers?

No, it does not.

Different approaches suit different people. Just like cooking a dish, there are many ways to achieve an outcome. Making a conscious decision on the way you want to be perceived by your team is an important step. Once you are clear on how you want them to see you, and believe this about yourself, your behaviour will start to align with this belief.

From a leadership training perspective, your initial behaviour starts to form new habits, which gives you a benchmark to return to under pressure, when most people forget to act and emotionally re-act to a circumstance.

So, think about how you want your team to describe your leadership style.

- What type of behaviour is consistent with that description?
- How would you like them to talk about you when you are not there?

- What kind of communication will get the best out of them?

Contact Time

As a father of two boys, there was always going to be a time when I'd be called upon as a volunteer coach. The local AFL club put us through a youth coaching program with the Essendon Bombers and their extended coaching team, which emphasised the importance of contact time with the team.

They explained that a head coach might have around 40 players in their charge, with multiple training sessions throughout the week – strength training, endurance work, skills practice – each with specialists. The coaching role needs to orchestrate the team's development to field their strongest team each week. The head coach explained that their one-to-one contact time with each individual was extremely limited – at times only 5 to 10 minutes a week. These are multimillion-dollar football teams in a high-stakes, elite competition. The coach emphasised that those conversations were absolutely pivotal to achieving targets and goals on the field.

Every word mattered.

One of my roles was as an executive chef with one of the country's largest pub and hotel operators, overseeing over 330 venues with a combined chef brigade of 1100. Due to the size and scope of the team, and logistics of getting to each venue, it became clear that my contact time with each head chef was going to be limited. I established a master class program and took it state by state, gathering all the head chefs together at key times throughout the year. This provided the opportunity for them to connect with each other and the business, to share knowledge on food standards and innovation. It was an action-packed immersive learning session, aiming to inspire the chefs into action. In a room of up to 80 people, the opportunity to be face-to-face with them might not re-occur for six months. This experience taught me the importance of making every word count – every point I made had to hit the mark, ensuring I could influence their behaviours and motivate them to act.

Let's say you had a team of ten staff on rotating shifts in a 7-day per week kitchen. In an ideal world, you'd spend the full day side-by-side with your team – but that's not realistic. After accounting for days off, shifts spread between prep, lunch and dinner, your actual contact time with key team members might come down to minutes in a day. How much time do you need with certain team members to develop their skills?

This is why your pre-service briefing and your post-service milk crate session are absolutely critical. They're the last words your staff member will take home with them at the end of the day to ponder overnight or on their days off. Any off-the-cuff remark or backhanded comment might not have the desired impact. It's important to consider what message you want them to hear.

People may not always remember exactly what you say, but they definitely remember how you make them feel.

Bean Therapy

In 2002 Jamie Oliver launched 'Fifteen' – a restaurant and social enterprise designed to train 15 disadvantaged, unemployed young people each year to become chefs. The candidates came from a range of varied backgrounds including homelessness, drug addiction and alcohol problems. The mission was to provide hospitality skills and inspire self-belief. Tobie Puttock opened the Melbourne branch in 2006, and I came on board as the training and development chef. If you know the TV series Jamie's Kitchen Australia, you'd appreciate the group we were working with didn't conform to traditional education or employment so needed a break. Everything was made in-house to showcase the best seasonal produce and build foundational cookery skills for the apprentices. In season, we'd have boxes of fresh broad beans delivered that needed to be prepared. It was quite the laborious task. I'd grab a few of our apprentices and put them to task podding the fresh broad beans. Keeping the hands busy while focusing on a set task allowed time to chat, while still being productive. These moments offered a chance to connect, listen, and share perspectives that could help shift their mindset. Contact time like this was rare in the busy kitchen, but it was profoundly meaningful. I found the apprentices were comfortable to share their journeys – what they were learning, loving or even struggling with.

Perhaps in your own journey, you've had someone who stood by your side to guide you through a task rather than leaving you to figure it out alone. That shared experience fosters rapport, builds trust and strengthens relationships – qualities that are invaluable in any team.

Learning Styles

Learning styles are a fascinating and essential consideration for any teacher, trainer, or leader. It's something I believe should get more attention in schools because it taps into how we, as humans, absorb and process information.

Here is a high-level breakdown of the four core learning styles:

(V) - Visual Learners

Ever heard the saying, *"A picture is worth a thousand words?"* For visual learners, this couldn't be truer — 80% of people fall into this category. They thrive on seeing information presented visually. A chart, photo, or example can spark instant understanding and action. The best way to communicate with these learners is by providing an image or diagram.

(A) - Auditory Learners

Auditory learners tune into words — what's being said and how it's delivered. They're the ones soaking up lessons from podcasts, reflecting on song lyrics and thriving in environments where verbal explanations are key. For them, the tone and rhythm of your voice can be just as impactful as the message itself. Repeating verbal instructions is a great way to communicate with an (A) learner.

(K) - Kinaesthetic Learners

Kinaesthetic learners are all about hands-on experience. They need to touch, feel, and do. These are the people who'll instinctively grab fresh produce, feel its texture or inhale its scent. In the kitchen, they're often the ones who thrive on action and engagement — and they might even greet you with a firm handshake or a hug because they connect through touch. Having something tactile is a great way to keep them engaged.

(Ad) - Auditory Digital Learners

Auditory Digital learners process information through internal dialogue. Instructions need to make sense and they have a tendency to bring their own logical order in the process. They observe, listen, or touch something and then engage in self-talk to make sense of it. You might catch them nodding subtly to themselves as they mentally agree with the information presented. Having them create their own notes, then recant the message back to you is a good way to communicate with an (Ad) learner.

While everyone uses all four learning styles, most of us have a strong default preference for one or two. Knowing these styles is crucial because it allows you to engage with your team more effectively when training them. Being aware of how your team best retain information allows you to share insights in a way that is meaningful for them. The kitchen, with its sensory-rich environment, is a perfect playground for learning. Think about it – you can show an ingredient (V), describe how it might be best to use it (A), pass it around for everyone to touch (K), smell, or taste, and then encourage a conversation (Ad) so each person can process the information provided and form their own understanding. This is why cookery training can be so impactful. You're engaging all the senses, making the learning process dynamic and memorable. It's also why cooking shows and masterclasses are so universally appealing – they hit every learning style in one well-orchestrated experience. As a leader in the kitchen, tapping into these learning styles doesn't just help your team grow; it creates a deeper connection, builds trust, and fosters a shared love for the craft.

Coaching vs Mentoring

I've been incredibly fortunate to learn from some amazing and talented people throughout my journey. The best lessons are usually the hardest ones, but having a supportive coach or mentor can make or break the quality of the learning experience. They play a crucial role in personal and professional growth and the relationships can last for many years, or a lifetime.

I've found great teachers fall into these three categories, with each one able to fast track your leadership journey.

Mentor

A mentor is someone who has walked in your shoes. They've experienced the challenges you're facing and can share insights about what worked for them in similar situations. A mentor offers perspective, wisdom, and guidance based on real-world experience, but it's up to you to decide whether to take their advice and apply it. Think of a mentor as someone who has 'been there, done that,' with a proven track record. They help you navigate your journey by sharing their own stories and lessons learned, offering you a valuable reference point as you tackle challenges.

Coach

A coach takes a different approach. They may not be an expert in your field, but they excel at helping you unlock your potential. Coaches are trained to ask the right questions, challenge your thinking, and push you to find solutions that align with your goals. Their focus isn't on telling you what to do but on empowering you to discover your own path and maximise your performance. A good coach gives you the tools and frameworks to grow, supporting you as you develop the confidence to make decisions and achieve results on your own. They will be your biggest supporter, and know how to encourage you to be the best version of yourself.

Virtual Mentor
With unlimited access to the internet, books, podcasts and social media, you can also learn from people you've never even met – I consider these virtual mentors. These are individuals whose wisdom and expertise you admire from afar. Maybe it's a chef whose cookbook you devour, a thought leader you follow on Instagram, or an entrepreneur whose biography you study. Virtual mentors allow you to tap into their experiences, learn from their successes and failures and apply those lessons to your own journey. While you may not know them personally, their insights can still shape your thinking and inspire your actions.

Understanding the differences between these roles – mentor, coach, and virtual mentor – helps you pinpoint the type of support you need at different stages of your leadership journey. Whether you're seeking practical advice, a performance boost, or inspiration, each has a unique role to play in helping you grow, lead, and thrive.

Key Chapter Takeaways

Communication as the core of leadership

Effective communication is essential for team engagement and leadership in the kitchen. Moments like milk crate sessions, pre-service briefings and post-service feedback are valuable opportunities to connect with the team, provide clarity and build trust. Leaders must plan their messages intentionally to ensure their words inspire action and align with team goals.

Building high-performance teams

A strong kitchen leader balances coaching and mentoring to unlock the potential of their team. Empowering team members to learn, grow and contribute leads to better performance, fosters collaboration and alleviates leadership burnout.

Leadership is a habit, not just a role

Small habits like daily greetings, offering feedback, and showing appreciation significantly impact workplace culture. Just like a dish is the sum of all the ingredients, small gestures don't go unnoticed and all contribute to creating an environment for your people to thrive.

Your Mise en Place

Complete these tasks to get the most out of this chapter...

➢ **Your support network**
Reflect on the coaches and mentors in your life. What kind of support do you need right now? What questions could you ask to gain clarity or direction? And just as importantly – how much time are you investing in mentoring your own team?

➢ **Contact time**
Map out your contact time with your key team members, considering the 1:1 time, informal conversations and de-briefing moments. Think about where you can direct your energy to have the greatest impact.

➢ **Sharpen your people skills**
If it's not already on your list, pick up *How to Win Friends and Influence People* by Dale Carnegie. It's a timeless guide to building genuine rapport – essential reading for any leader building trust and connection.

> **Lead with Intention**
> Each day, take a moment to reflect: How are you showing up? Are your words, tone, and body language aligned with the leader you want to be? Are you reacting to the chaos, or responding with calm, focused intention?

Chapter 2

Can You Handle the Heat?

Emotion

"Cooking for a living, at any level is a tough, uncomfortable, high pressure business."
   - Heston Blumenthal

A commercial kitchen, as a workplace environment, is not for everyone. From an occupational health and safety perspective every piece of equipment wants to do you harm. Sharp edges, slippery floors, smoking hot grills to the infamous meat slicer – it's a regular chop shop. And that's on a good day!

You may have heard the saying, 'If you can't take the heat get out of the kitchen'. But if you're reading this book, chances are you're already committed to the journey. Over the last 10-15 years the pathways to earn a living in the food industry have significantly increased. Shows like MasterChef have opened the consumers appetite for ingredients and with that marketing budgets, social media campaigns and content creation. There is a buzz and energy around food that makes it an exciting industry for those who are motivated.

There are so many translatable skills to be learned in a kitchen environment. Service is a crash course in life skills – teaching, planning, communication, creativity, teamwork, organisation, time management, prioritisation, adaptability and resilience all at once. The pressure is constant, forcing you to stay calm and think clearly when the heat is on.

Taking it one step further – the mindful act of cooking is not to be underestimated. Cooking isn't just about feeding yourself or others – it's a way to connect with the moment in a world that pulls us in every direction. When in the midst of a making a dish, you're completely tuned in – it's like a state of flow. Smoking pan, seared scallops, blanching asparagus, emulsifying butter and herbs, preparing the plate, assembling the ingredients while timing with the other sections, all following the rhythm of service.

In those moments, there's no room for white noise, no distractions – just you, your tools and the ingredients. For many home cooks, the craft of cooking invites them to slow down, focus and savour being fully present – following a recipe through to deliver something nourishing to friends or family.

Consistency Through Chaos

In this chapter we're going to cover emotional regulation. In order to be a leader of others, you first must be in control of yourself. The benefits of this topic are far-reaching. Understanding how your emotions play a role will help reduce stress levels and keep you calm under pressure, to think clearer and make better decisions. You'll come across more controlled, measured and logical which is essential to leading a team.

Customer demands bring enough deadlines and pressure into the equation, without you adding more into the mix. Calm staff work more productively and have longer tenure.

A number of studies highlight the significant stress chefs endure due to long working hours and demanding job conditions. In 2020 a study of over 700 Italian chefs rated the stress levels of chefs equal with those of police officers and paramedics. In 2023, Auckland University and Queensland University completed an Australasian Study of the mental health and wellbeing of chefs. The study reported many characteristics associated with poor lifestyle and health habits, including elevated rates of daily drinking, low rates of overall individual wellbeing, lower than average resilience and poor quality sleep.

Identifying stress triggers and having a number of coping strategies is important for your ability to perform.

A normal day in the kitchen 'office' can turn into a roller coaster of intensity. There are so many elements beyond your control – supplier deliveries running late, the weather, produce not available, staff calling in sick, last-minute booking changes, suppliers dropping in for an unscheduled meeting, equipment malfunction. Add in mise en place and service and you've got a pretty full agenda.

Time is such a critical obsession that chefs need to be across.

It's the Customer, Right?

You see chefs run on a micro time. Seconds count when you are dealing with such delicate and highly perishable produce. Five seconds can mean the difference between perfectly cooked and overdone. These finite deadlines are not for the faint-hearted. There is a certain match fitness that comes with the territory, which is learned over time. You just need the persistence to go through the paces. In his book *Uses for Obsession*, Ben Shewry of Attica states "Cooking for a living is like a marathon runner who runs a four-hour sprint to arrive at the starting banner, then runs the marathon".

Each dish brings a new set of deadlines. The protein, vegetables, garnish, sauce, seasoning… every element needs to come together simultaneously, within a few seconds to create a great dish and meet the customer expectations. In essence, every meal is a project deadline.

Consider the math.

Eight items being assembled on the plate, within five to ten seconds. Each one pan fried, seasoned, warmed, scorched or simmered. That's one customer.

Can You Handle the Heat?

Table of four? 32 items, all coming together, within a window of seconds, from a team of varied skill sets, cultural backgrounds, nationalities, perhaps languages, in a pressure cooker environment. The mind boggles.

And that's just one table. Say there is 120 booked for lunch? And 160 for dinner. Every. Single. Day.

While a builder might go a few weeks over a deadline, or a mechanic keep your vehicle overnight because they 'didn't get to it', the impact of a failed deadline for a chef is immediate.

The upset customer shares their emotion with the front of house staff, who feed it back into the kitchen. It's a bitter pill to swallow when you're 20 dockets deep and trying to please everyone. It's easy to head home that night obsessing over that one customer who was upset their steak was overcooked, discounting the other 100 people who seemed happy, paid their bill and left without a fuss.

The Illusion of Control

As a human you are a beautifully perfect bundle of emotions, set to react or respond to certain events. As a kitchen leader the first thing you need to do is understand yourself and know your trigger points. Bringing awareness to these emotions means that they're no longer operating in your subconscious – they are front and centre for you to see, reflect on and understand.

We've all been on the pass when a dish is returned. In that moment, there is no time for a committee meeting to discuss the customer's perspective. The emotional response could be frustration, disappointment, fury, despair or anger. This all happens instantaneously and can shift your mood in a heartbeat.

Response 1: Emotion takes control and it looks like an episode of Hell's Kitchen. All of a sudden the waiter is getting berated, the customer (not even in earshot) is also described in colourful language and the returned dish is thrown in the bin. This split-second response now causes further, separate issues. The dish needs replacing, the waiter needs to speak with the customer, the team are plating the next table and another staff member who observed the altercation is a bit rattled. All this takes about 20 seconds.

Response 2: Emotion kicks in. A breath is taken to consider options. The dish is taken and the waiter advised – 'give me a few minutes'. The chef checks the estimated time of a replacement meal from the team, remains calm while communicating this information to the waitstaff, realising that re-acting in a poor way here can disrupt the focus of the service. Chef then proceeds plating the next table. The rhythm of service continues un-interrupted.

Emotions are neither right nor wrong. They are hardwired into the human response system and a normal part of a functioning person. The more aware you are of what drives you and what gets under your skin, the better chance you've got of harnessing the right emotions at the right time – or simply doing nothing. The small gap or pause gives enough time to consider alternative perspectives and make a logical decision that is not emotionally charged. Too many chefs get swept up in the adrenaline rollercoaster – riding the highs, crashing with the lows.

Take 4 Seconds

In his book, *Four Seconds* author and productivity expert Peter Bregman shows us how to replace negative patterns with better decision-making and productive behaviours in a fast-paced environment. Pausing for the length of a deep breath allows you to make intentional and considered choices that lead to better outcomes. It's a powerful strategy that is simple to understand and simple to implement. Before making an immediate response, take a breath and just consider the outcomes. Resist the urge to immediately roll up the sleeves, dive in and problem-solve. While being the hero of the moment might feel amazing, a good leader has the ability to slightly slow things down and be more measured and more controlled. This allows the team to learn. Something as simple as taking a deep breath really works.

I know some of us have a short fuse and prefer to unleash a verbal spray, enjoying the rush of endorphins associated with venting anger. This might be fine as a young hot head, but as a senior team member all it does is show that you're out of your depth and have no control over your emotions.

The team, business and customer all suffer. Everyone handles pressure differently and understanding your own emotions and how they show up in certain situations is the first step.

Think about what we say when planning out a meal: "What do you *feel* like tonight?" That simple question is packed with emotion. It's not logical – it's not "I need to eat pulled pork". It's instinctive, personal, and subjective.

As a kitchen leader, your role is to interpret that feeling. You take a mood, a craving, a moment – and translate it through the menu, through the pass, into the hands of your team, and finally onto the plate. Your aim? To satisfy something intangible.

Get it right – happy customers. But miss the mark?....... how many times have you heard, *"Ohh - that's not what I expected"*.

This industry is fraught with danger. This makes it challenging but also exhilarating.

Just take a deep breath.

Act vs Re-act

In the chaos of a busy kitchen, your approach to handling pressure can set the tone for everything – and everyone – around you. Acting is about staying grounded, thinking ahead and making intentional decisions. It's the calm and collected chef who sees the big picture, anticipates challenges and keeps their team moving forward. Reacting, on the other hand, is letting the stress take over – snapping at a chef over a burned steak or scrambling to fix a botched order without a plan. Reacting is impulsive, and while it might feel like you're addressing the issue in the moment, it often makes things worse.

Can You Handle the Heat?

The key difference between acting and reacting comes down to one simple but powerful thing: the pause. When something goes sideways – and let's face it, in a kitchen, it frequently does – how you respond in those first few seconds matter. Taking a moment to breathe, assess the situation, and decide how you want to handle it gives you control over the outcome. It's not about ignoring the chaos; it's about stepping back enough to think clearly.

When you lead with composure, your team will follow suit. If they see you keeping it together under pressure, it inspires confidence and helps them focus. But if you're flying off the handle, yelling or getting emotional, that energy spreads like wildfire. The kitchen mirrors its leader. By choosing to act instead of react, you're setting the standard for professionalism and remaining calm, no matter how intense things get.

This isn't just about managing the kitchen better – it's about creating an environment where your team feels supported and respected. A calm leader fosters a calm crew, and that's when the real magic happens. Orders flow out seamlessly, mistakes are handled with composure, and everyone walks out of service feeling like they have contributed and achieved.

Key Chapter Takeaways

Emotional awareness

Understanding your emotions and their triggers can help you reduce stress and stay in control during high-pressure situations. Recognising how emotions influence your decisions allows for more measured and thoughtful responses.

The power of the pause

A simple four-second pause, paired with intentional breathing, can interrupt impulsive reactions, helping you respond thoughtfully instead of emotionally. This small but effective technique allows better decisions to be made.

Tailored support

Not everyone handles pressure the same way. Observing and understanding how your team members react under stress enables you to offer the right kind of support, helping them – and your kitchen – perform at their best.

Your Mise en Place

Complete these tasks to get the most out of this chapter...

➢ **Daily reflection**
Keep a journal for one week. Each night, write down the emotions you experienced, what triggered them, and how you reacted. At the end of the week review your notes to identify patterns and areas for growth. If this activity is helpful, continue it for a month.

➢ **Use the 4-second rule**
When emotions run high, pause. Inhale for four seconds, exhale for four seconds. This simple breathing pattern helps create space between stimulus and response. Over time, you'll notice how it subtly shifts your reactions.

➢ **Add to your toolkit**
Add *Four Seconds: All the Time You Need to Replace Counter-Productive Habits with Ones That Really Work* by Peter Bregman to your reading or listening list. Look for a few bite-sized ideas you can apply straight away in your kitchen leadership.

Chapter 3

Fuelling the Fire

Energy

"A recipe has no soul. You, as the cook, must bring soul to the recipe."
- Thomas Keller

Sustainability is a subject that's heavily talked about in the food industry. Understandably, it's a highly emotional topic that gets thrown around frequently in the media, especially when it comes to food production.

But deeper than just food production, leading a kitchen team crosses into these 3 areas:

1. Environmental Sustainability – care for the planet.
2. Economical Sustainability – care for the cash flow.
3. Personal Sustainability – care for yourself.

Let's break down these areas at a high level.

Environmental Sustainability

In the establishment you're running they should have some form of environmental sustainability plan or philosophy in place, which not only ties in with the business direction but also looks at systems to maximise yield and reduce wastage. Some operators move beyond the kitchen into recycled or repurposed materials, eclectic plates, reusing ground coffee for compost, ethical sourcing, purchasing from local suppliers to reduce food miles, energy consumption to reduce carbon footprint, repurposing organic waste or sending useable food to charity organisations. I'm not going to dive too deep into this as it's a conversation in its own right, but you get the idea.

If there is nothing currently in place, what questions can you ask the business owner or leadership team to guide their thinking and play the bigger game? It does not have to be a huge undertaking or trying to change the world. Even a few small, adjusted habits have long-term impacts in your own backyard.

- What materials could be recycled into the local community?
- What food waste is going through your bins that is unnecessary, and could be skilfully repurposed for another dish?
- What local suppliers are you working with?

- What seasonal produce is being utilised in your menu?

Economic Sustainability

All of the positive intention to care for the planet and supporting ethical producers means nothing if you have to close your doors and shut the business. When you purchase produce via unit and weight, being financially savvy and resourceful is an important factor in running a food business. Monitoring cash flow and staying in business ensures your team are employed and their families are provided for.

Many of the hospitality operators I work with talk about the responsibility they feel for not only their team, but the livelihoods of their families and children. There's an old adage, 'If you look after the pennies, the pounds look after themselves'. If you want to make a difference, ultimately you need to stay in the game. Economic sustainability will enhance your financial literacy and is covered in more detail within the next few chapters.

Personal Sustainability

Your personal energy is a critical factor in having a long and rewarding career in hospitality. I think this is the most important of the three. Have you ever heard of the term R.O.I. or Return On Investment? It's a performance measure used to evaluate the viability of investments and determine what is the best potential bang for your buck.

In a personal sense, I like to think of this in terms of R.O.E – Return On Energy. Where are you investing your time and heartbeats in terms of your business, your team, your family and yourself?

The purpose of developing your kitchen leadership capability is to not simply survive but ultimately thrive in a very dynamic, fluid and challenging environment. What's on offer within this chapter is for you to understand how you can leverage your energy each day.

A Balanced Diet

Jamie's Kitchen Australia was a 10-part TV series that premiered in September 2006, following the personal journey of the first intake of apprentices and the opening of the restaurant 'Fifteen Melbourne'.

I was in charge of training and development, and it was one of the most dynamic and rewarding roles that I've ever had. I had not come from a traditional teaching background, which was perfect for the cohort we were working with. I held nothing back, pouring my heart and soul into building the training program, because I believed in the difference we were making with our young recruits. I knew I was out of my depth but pushed on regardless.

Looking back, I was suffering from 'impostor syndrome' and so far outside of my comfort zone when trying to engage, teach and mentor 20 young people to give them the tools and the techniques they needed to survive in the kitchen environment. Factoring in their personal backgrounds and my lack of experience dealing with their daily challenges, I didn't fully consider the energetic and emotional toll that the role was going to take on me.

Fuelling the Fire

My desire to help and support was over-indexed and I didn't know how to slow down or take a break. The apprentices were on my mind 24/7. It was all-consuming.

After working with the Fifteen Foundation for almost three years, I was exhausted. I'd burned out a few times along the way, but I believed in the program and believed in the work we were all doing for a great group of young people. During this time my wife had also given birth to our first son. For any first-time parents reading this – you can appreciate the time vortex that can send you into. Niki turned to me one day in the midst of my exhaustion and simply stated, "Glenn, you remind me of a sandcastle....every day the water laps up against it and just a little bit more has gone". Her words hit home and provided me with a powerful lesson.

Sometimes chefs get so caught up in the whirlwind of their work – focusing on their passion for food, driving their team and going above and beyond for their customers – that they forget to pause and recalibrate. The intense, all-consuming nature of the job can make it feel like an 'all-in' affair. But failing to find time to step back and recharge, often leads to one inevitable outcome: burnout.

Going all in usually equals being all out in a short period of time.

Switch Off
Everyone replenishes their energy in different ways. Having the ability to switch off, to put things down, to defrag, recharge, is important for a leader to know. For some, it's

putting their feet up on the beach, going for a massage, meditation, getting some exercise, going fishing or playing a round of golf. There are so many options to consider.

Mindfulness plays very heavily in this space – or as I prefer to think of it, mind-less-ness.

Know the activities that replenish you and make you feel good. It does not have to be a huge investment of time (like an overseas holiday); sometimes just a walk in nature, reading a book, capturing your thoughts in a journal or walking the dog is enough to ensure you stay grounded.

Switching off is crucial – not just for your mental well-being but for your physical health too. Activities that release endorphins and dopamine, like exercise, are a natural and healthy way to recharge. Team sports, for instance, are fantastic because they provide both physical activity and a commitment to something outside of work. In a trade that is physically demanding and all-encompassing, if you want to sustain your health and energy, finding that balance is essential.

Taking time for self-care doesn't have to be overwhelming. It's not about hitting the gym five days a week or running a marathon. Start small. Maybe it's one walk, one afternoon for yourself, or even just one single push-up. Start small, then build.

Day 1 – 1 push-up, Day 2 – 2 push-ups…..Day 3 – you get the picture. Then, as you keep going day by day, those small habits will build. Before you know it, you're doing 50, 100 push-ups, or whatever feels right for you.

These small, consistent actions accumulate over time. Like brushing your teeth, you will not see instant results, but imagine if you neglected to do it for a month, or a year? At the end of the day, your health is your greatest asset. Keeping your energy and fitness levels up not only helps you sustain the demands of the job but also allows you to bring your best self to your team and your work every single day.

Workin' 9 to 5

In the hospitality industry, we operate in a space where customer expectations are relentless. People eat seven days a week – breakfast, lunch, dinner and often snacks in between. While this creates constant demand, it doesn't mean you need to cater for every single mealtime. Review your core market, their needs and spending patterns and understand your goals from a business perspective – then align your efforts accordingly.

By narrowing your focus, you can set up rosters that work for your team and yourself. Strive for schedules that allow for proper downtime, ensuring everyone gets the chance to recharge. Balance is crucial – consider blending weekends off or structuring additional days together on a fortnightly or monthly basis. Gone are the days of six double shifts a week. That approach is unsustainable and ultimately harmful for everyone involved.

Looking after your team requires providing them with a genuine work-life balance. Breaks should be meaningful, offering time to reset. Why not make those moments engaging? Encourage movement, camaraderie and energy during downtime. Place a deck of cards, interesting books, a frisbee or ping-pong table into the staff area. Small touches like these show you care about the well-being of your team and promote engagement.

Think of your career as a long game. Just as elite athletes need to manage their physicality to perform consistently at the top level, so do chefs. Acknowledge the physical toll of the trade and pace yourself.

Equally important is preparing for the different phases of your career. By managing your energy and developing your skills, you'll not only stay in the game longer but also build the tools you need to explore new opportunities as your career evolves. Prioritising balance and sustainability isn't just good for today — it sets you up for a fulfilling, lifelong career in the food industry.

Remember, you've already invested years in honing your craft — perfecting techniques, understanding ingredients and delivering consistent dishes. Leadership is no different; it's a skill that takes time, practice and personal growth to develop. Don't expect to master it overnight. But with effort and persistence, it's entirely within reach.

TGI Fridays

While working with the Fifteen Foundation, I had the opportunity to deliver a keynote presentation on *'Innovation in Education'* to over 350 teachers and educators. The event was scheduled for 3.00pm on a Friday afternoon, and though I didn't realise it at the time, I was to be the final speaker of a three-day conference.

Fuelling the Fire

Arriving early, I slipped into the back of the conference to get a sense of the audience and a read on the room. It was like an energy vacuum. It was clear the group were beyond fatigue. The back-to-back sessions had taken their toll.

Three days of this? I thought – that's exhausting. I knew I had to step away for a moment because I could feel myself being pulled into their energy drain, and that wouldn't help me deliver the keynote I was about to give. My talk, titled "People, Passion, Produce," was all about exploring the emotional connection people have with food as a way to boost student engagement. I needed to bring my A-game.

I did my best to keep my energy high, set up for the presentation, and prepared to launch my 'intro reel' – a high-impact visual designed to set the tempo and grab the audience's attention. But just as I was about to begin, the tech team dropped the ball. The screen went blank.

Awkward silence followed.

I now had 700 weary eyes staring at me. I could hear my heart beating loudly, and my temperature increasing. It was like tripping over your shoelaces and falling flat on your face at the start of a marathon, with the crowd looking on.

It was a tough moment, which seemed to stretch for hours. I could feel the blood draining from my face and could see the empathy on the people in the front few rows.

Deep breath. Improvise.

"Shit, that's pretty awkward – I'd hate to be me right now," I managed to blurt out...

Laughter – the energy in the room shifted, my confidence returned and I got the job done.

After the keynote many of the attendees came up to thank me stating – "We should have opened the conference with you – that was uplifting, so insightful...Thank you!"

The impact your energy has over your mindset is not to be underplayed. You need good positive energy to be at your creative best, to build team momentum and create a dynamic that people will buy into.

Leadership is about how you make those around you feel, how you connect with them on an energetic level and how you can inspire them to perform. Your tone and communication levels are important factors to achieve this. What you say and how you say it.

Work and Life Integration
Work-life balance can be hard to achieve because life rarely unfolds in neat, predictable ways. Work demands often clash with personal responsibilities, especially when trading seven days a week, in a high-pressure environment with an irregular schedule.

Technology makes it even tougher, with emails and messages pinging 24/7. Your phone reminds you, 'This week you averaged 6 hours and 27 minutes screen time each day'.

Fuelling the Fire

'Off the clock' time can feel non-existent. For many, the idea of balance implies an equal split, which can be unrealistic when urgent deadlines or life events arise. If a chef calls in sick, it directly affects the customer, brand and financial performance of the business. Add to that the emotional investment people put into their careers, and it's easy for work to take over. The challenge is finding a sustainable rhythm that respects both professional goals and personal well-being.

Work-life integration is often considered better because it reflects the reality of modern life, where the boundaries between work and personal time are increasingly blurred. Instead of trying to separate work and life into rigid compartments, integration focuses on blending the two in a way that feels natural and manageable. For example, you might take a personal call during a work break or tackle some tasks from home while spending time with family. This approach allows more flexibility, reduces the pressure to achieve 'perfect balance,' and lets you align your work with your personal values and priorities. It can be a more sustainable and fulfilling way to manage responsibilities.

Kitchen leadership is not about being a workaholic. Planning where your time is best invested is absolutely critical to long-term sustainability for your energy. Here are some simple ideas to help you.

- Plan your week carefully, scheduling time for yourself first, next your direct reports, and then the items that are most important. If your week was a glass jar, put the big rocks in first.

- If you are building a new team, your time is best spent with the new team members, onboarding them to the standards and understanding their capability.
- Remember that working the most hours is not a badge of honour.
- Set micro goals and celebrate them often – people love progression.
- Be disciplined with your time. Putting your health and yourself last in line is a fast track to burnout.
- Remember it's just food – not brain surgery. No one is going to die if things are not perfect. Keep life in perspective.

Phone a Friend

Surrounding yourself with great people and a strong inner circle is a fast track to success. Entrepreneur and author Jim Rohn famously stated, "You are the average of the five people you spend the most amount of time with". Now that can be a very interesting thought!

Have you ever conducted a stocktake on who you are spending time with?

Millionaire Hot Seat is a TV game show where the contestant is asked a series of questions to win cash prizes. As they progress, the money increases and so does the intensity of the questions. But the contestant has a lifeline – when they are not 100% sure about an answer, they can ask to 'phone a friend' for advice. This is a powerful concept.

Think about your top five friends or colleagues...the ones who are always excited to hear from you, always good energy, happy to offer a fresh perspective or be a sympathetic ear. Have these people on your speed dial and utilise them strategically.

The thinking that got you into a challenging situation is not the same level of thinking you need to get out of it. So, when you are harnessing the energy and knowledge from someone you trust, it makes all the difference for you to work through the challenge.

Upgrade Your Habits

Studies in neurology indicate that (on average) a new habit takes 66 days to be hardwired into your subconscious so that you're in a state of automaticity. It's like muscle memory when you're learning how to dice an onion. The first few might be a little bit slow, but after 5-10 kilos you are more efficient. When you conduct the task day in and day out for a couple of months you can simply pick up an onion, have it peeled, halved, sliced and diced without even thinking about it.

In his book *Atomic Habits*, author James Clear emphasises how good and bad habits can impact your routine and even the smallest changes can end up providing massive results in the long-term. Clear encourages the reader to focus on systems, as opposed to goal-setting. He argues that goal-setting can give you direction, but systems allow you to embed the habits required to attain the goal, which is far more effective for long-term results.

This poses the question about prioritising tasks that make you happy. When was the last time you carved out time each day or each week to spend time doing the things that you really want to do? Connecting with the outdoors, walking in nature, going for a bike ride, fishing, gardening, cooking for family, firing up the smoker, playing sports, watching movies, listening to music, chatting with a loved one or catching up with friends??

Installing productive habits into your schedule is a game-changer. Much in the same way that chefs set their station before service, having the mise en place in place for a personally rewarding activity reduces friction and makes the task easier to obtain, and with it the positive payoff. Like having a gym bag packed the night prior so the early start requires zero effort.

What habits are holding you back?

Pursue Your Passion

I know, this sounds a little bit cheesy as chefs are always asked to express their passion for food, for ingredients, for the craft of cooking. It's easy to get sucked into the process of cooking, absorbed in the daily pressures of customers, reviews, bookings, team challenges, timing, training, food cost and labour controls.

When was the last time you slowed down to really appreciate the simple act of cooking? Or walk through a vegetable garden, or visit a deli just for your own enjoyment? No time pressure, no customer expectation. Just refuelling your passion for your craft?

Fuelling the Fire

Passion is what takes over when fatigue kicks in.

It's the element that is essential in any field to operate at a high level. There may have been a time or a moment when the joy of cooking first grabbed your attention. The creative pursuit and discovery of flavours – like a child the first time tasting ice cream.

Successful chefs draw joy from the basic and simple kitchen tasks. Filleting a fish, peeling a potato, washing herbs, searing a steak…. Preparing food to nourish another person is a wonderful act, so enjoy that aspect of it. Countless studies in the field of positive psychology support the idea that acts of kindness and gratitude are powerful tools to sustain a positive mindset.

If you can unlock the joy in tasks or jobs to the extent that you would do them just for the sheer pleasure, then that is a definition of success.

The pursuit of passion can sometimes be fragile in the kitchen, and can be exploited if not protected. Passion can quickly burn out if it's drained by long hours, relentless stress, or an environment that takes more than it gives.

Protecting your passion means setting boundaries and making space to reconnect with why you started your food journey in the first place. It means finding moments of inspiration, whether through experimenting with new flavours, learning from peers, or simply stepping away to recharge. Nurture your passion, because it's the fuel that keeps the fire alive, even in the most challenging of times.

Key Chapter Takeaways

Take care of yourself first

Think of your energy like a bank account. You can't keep making withdrawals without making deposits. Burnout is real in this industry, so focus on what keeps you going – whether it's exercise, mindfulness, hobbies, or just a walk in nature. Little habits add up over time, and your well-being is what keeps you in the game.

The goal is not simply surviving – it's thriving.

Find a work-life flow

The kitchen never sleeps, but that doesn't mean you have to be on 24/7. Create a schedule that works for you and your team, with enough downtime to recharge. Leadership isn't about working the most hours; it's about working smart, playing the long game and showing up in good form.

Keep the passion alive

Your passion for cooking is what got you here – but it's fragile. Protect it at all costs. Make time to rekindle the fire. Keep it burning by giving yourself the space to reconnect with why you started this journey.

Your Mise en Place

Complete these tasks to get the most out of this chapter...

➤ **Schedule yourself first**
Look for ways to incorporate more 'you' into your daily schedule. Plan your day around the activities that make you feel most energised. This helps maintain a sustainable work-life integration and prevents burnout.

➤ **Rate your energy levels**
Track your energy levels at the same time each day for two weeks on a scale from 1 to 10. Note the activity you did, who you interacted with, and what external factors affect your energy. By identifying patterns, you can adjust your schedule to maintain your ideal energy levels throughout the day.

➤ **Identify when you feel at your best**
Pay attention to when you feel most focused and energised. What thoughts or feelings contribute to this? *(This is an extension of rate your energy levels.)* It could be after walking the dog, quality sleep, crafting a new dish, helping a friend or spending time outdoors. Look for achievable daily tasks. Construct this into a 'energy hack' list and use the activities to pick you up when you need.

The Second Mastery

Finance

Chapter 4

Beyond the Menu

Positioning

"As the leader, it is up to me to set the game plan – to articulate my vision, to guide, inspire and keep the team focused."
- Charlie Trotter

As a chef, you know it's never just about the food – it's about the entire guest experience, from the moment they book a table, through to the last bite of dessert – every interaction leaves an impression. Their expectations, the first contact upon arrival, the energy and ambience of the room, or the dishes you've crafted with care. That's the customer journey. It's your responsibility to make sure every touchpoint is memorable for the right reasons.

In this chapter, we'll dive into why the customer journey matters and how to strike the perfect balance between delivering on expectations and meeting the needs of your business. You'll learn how to use storytelling to create meaningful connections and how to align the menu with your food philosophy, creating the right position within the local market.

What's the Story?

One of the most powerful ways to connect your brand with customers from an emotional perspective is through sharing stories. There are multiple platforms from which you can curate and share the story on. LinkedIn, Instagram, Facebook, websites, podcast interviews and industry publications are all great options once you are clear on the story.

I have worked with some legends in the culinary field (as well as some imposters!) and the ones who consistently grow in influence each year with their business, engagement, support and legacy are those who are clear on their unique perspective. They are not chasing trends, yelling from the soap box or trying to force their view down your throat. They are the real deal and have a story that their followers can relate to and buy into.

Some of these high-profile chefs have had help along the way, leveraging off PR firms and using talent management companies to broker larger deals. It's exciting to consider the variety of ways chefs and foodies can ply their craft in today's economy. The high performers are always consistent in their message and usually very humble to have such a connected audience who share their food values.

Beyond the Menu

Here is where some deep thinking is required from you. Answering these questions will help to clarify your ideas and commence crafting your unique perspective.

My suggestion is to not overthink the initial answers. The best results come from having a go and trusting your 'gut feel'. If you already have formed an opinion in these areas, have someone ask you these questions and see if the response has evolved or shifted:

1. What do you love to cook the most, and why?
2. Who has inspired your career so far?
3. When did you first fall into cooking as a career?
4. What is your most memorable food experience?
5. When you need to impress — where do you look for inspiration?
6. How would others describe you as a chef?
7. What words come to mind when asked to explain your food philosophy?

Answering these questions will allow your stories and ideas to start to flow. Take your time and remember the details surrounding each answer, where you were, who you were with, what you were feeling and capture that moment. This level of deep thinking will underpin your ethos toward food and start to bring structure to how you share that message across your biography, resume, website or social media platforms.

In his cookbook *Origin*, Ben Shewry gives a raw and honest account of his food philosophy. He writes, *"My food has been described as narrative food and in many aspects that's a correct description. Almost all my dishes are inspired by an important memory, story or past experience..........With everything I do at Attica I'm attempting to bring food back to its rawest form and to reconnect with nature and cultural history."*

Even in such a short statement you can get a feel for the building blocks he uses when creating a menu item, training his team to understand the dishes or talking about his cuisine.

It all begins with a good story.

Eat Local

For most hospitality businesses, 80% of customers come from within a 5-kilometre radius. This local catchment means that building a reputation for consistency and a clear identity is crucial for long-term success. In markets like clubs and pubs, loyalty is often tied to convenience and familiarity. Customers stick with you because you're nearby, dependable and make them feel connected. Your role is to give them every reason to keep coming back, meeting their expectations and occasionally surprising them with something new.

Many customers have grown up in the area and are very familiar with the reputation. They know what to expect, and if you deliver a comfortable and reliable experience, you've got the foundation of a great business. Food lovers willing to cross town for a unique dining adventure are usually the exception, not the rule – unless your venue offers something truly extraordinary or fills a distinct niche that sets it apart from competitors.

It's important to understand your core customers and tailor the offer to their needs. One way to achieve this is by analysing your menu sales. Simple data can reveal what works. 80% of your revenue often comes from just 20% of the items on the menu. These will all be top sellers. Make sure these items have standard recipes, are correctly portioned, weighed and costed to maintain profitability while consistently meeting customer expectations.

When you cater to the local market, you're not just serving food, you're reinforcing a sense of community and belonging. By refining your offerings and focusing on what matters most to your customers, you set yourself up for sustainable commercial success while making your mark in the local dining scene.

Positioning
Understanding how your food business fits into the market matters on three levels:

1. Business
This is the big-picture strategy – how your restaurant or café views itself. Are you a casual local spot or a fine-dining destination? Maybe you're all about quick, quality takeout or a farm-to-table experience. Whatever it is, your business plan needs to define your identity clearly, so you can focus on what you do best.

2. Customer
This is about perception – how your customers see you. What makes your place unique? Why do they choose you

over someone else? A clear identity helps you build loyalty and trust, so your customers know exactly what to expect every time they walk in.

3. Self
Here's where you, as the kitchen leader, tie it all together. Your job is to align the business strategy with customer expectations, and your main tool for doing this is the menu. It's not just a list of dishes, it's your key sales tool, your storytelling medium, and the driving force behind your cash flow. A well-positioned menu can make or break your success.

When these three areas are in sync, everything clicks. You attract the right crowd, deliver consistent experiences, and set your venue up for long-term success.

Food Philosophy
Your food philosophy is your culinary north star. It showcases your ideas, shapes your menu content and gives the customers insight into your values. It doesn't just reflect your personal style; it should align with the broader business goals, creating a seamless and memorable dining experience.

It defines what you believe about food and ensures every decision you make supports that belief. Whether you're running a casual café, a fine-dining establishment, or a takeaway outlet, your philosophy shapes your identity and keeps you focused. It also provides a benchmark of criteria when developing prospective new dishes.

Here are a few well-curated examples:

> "I'm inspired by nature and have coined the term 'Nature-based cuisine' to describe my food. Nature offers us so much diversity – a natural elegance and beauty, and it is the organic nature of food, its textures and flavours that is at the heart of my cooking."
>
> **– Peter Gilmore, Quay**

> "Margaret is a neighbourhood restaurant, but it's also evolved into something more than that. At its core, it's about comfort, generosity and cosiness."
>
> **– Neil Perry, Margaret**

> "It's our house, but more so, it's your home. A place to come often, it's warm and authentic, but above all it's deliciously Greek."
>
> **– George Calombaris, Hellenic House Project**

Creating your food philosophy starts with reflection and discussion. Here's a process that has worked for many chefs and businesses I've worked with:

Understand the business identity: For many chefs, stepping into a leadership role means inheriting an existing business identity. Before making changes, ask about the vision and positioning. What's the owner's goal? What's the brand known for? For example, a local pizza shop should focus on casual, family-friendly offerings, not high-priced fine dining. Aligning with the existing identity avoids mixed messaging and confusion for the customer.

Ask questions: Hold a session with key stakeholders and explore questions like:

- What does food and dining mean to us?
- What emotions or memories do we want to evoke?
- How do we want our customers to feel?
- What do we want to be known for?
- What values underpin the food we serve?

Identify key themes: Through discussion, identify the core words that represent your food philosophy. Aim to boil these down to three or four key themes so they are easy to remember.

Here are a few examples:

Seasonality: Highlighting fresh, in-season produce
Local: Partnering with nearby farms or artisan producers
Authentic: Staying true to traditions
Generosity: On the plate, going above and beyond with service
Fun: Energetic, playful, engaging

Make it practical: A philosophy isn't just an idea, it's a guide for action. If 'local sourcing' is a theme, then prioritise local suppliers. If 'comfort food' is important to you, ensure your menu reflects it. Make sure your ideas are not just buzzwords and see them through.

Why it Matters
Having a clear food philosophy is practical and powerful. Here's why:

Menu Planning – Your philosophy helps determine what dishes belong on your menu and ensures a common thread. Avoid the trap of trying to please everyone – focus on what aligns with your core themes and give it every chance to succeed.

Purchasing Decisions – The philosophy guides your supplier relationships, building the framework of your supplier ecosystem and your selection of ingredients. If you purchase top quality ingredients, the menu should reflect that in the prices. If your customers will not pay the asking price, revisit the overall philosophy.

Customer Expectations – A clear philosophy ensures guests know what to expect. Meeting these expectations builds trust and loyalty, the cornerstone of a good customer base.

What's on the Menu?
Think of your menu as your primary sales tool. It's not just about showcasing your creativity; it's about meeting the market's needs while maintaining your identity.

Consider these steps before overhauling a menu:

- Review historical sales data to understand what's working.
- Gather customer feedback to identify popular dishes.

- Align with the skill level of your team and available equipment.
- Check the firepower of your cook line during peak trade.
- Incorporate insights from long-term staff and owners.

Inexperienced chefs often rush to change everything, leading to unnecessary friction. Experienced chefs take a strategic approach, making incremental changes that involve the team and reflect the business's food philosophy.

Let's Grab Lunch

Great kitchen leaders take the time to consider every aspect of the customer journey. I had the privilege of working in the UK with Michelin-starred French chef Daniel Galmiche. Daniel's career had taken him all around the world, and in London at the highly acclaimed *'Le Gavroche'* with Albert and Michel Roux. His industry peers and friends include the likes of Heston Blumenthal (The Fat Duck), Raymond Blanc (Le Manoir aux Quat'Saisons) and Gordon Ramsay (Restaurant Gordon Ramsay).

Each month, during his day off Daniel would drop by the kitchen at Harvey's, Bristol, to enjoy a meal in the dining room. He taught me that it's vital to experience the dishes from the customer's perspective, rather than getting caught up in what we (as chefs) see on the pass. *"The meal transforms entirely on the dining room floor".*

A simple yet powerful idea.

Beyond the Menu

The customer doesn't see the effort, focus, technique, mise en place, brunoise of shallots, chlorophyll extraction, reductions, overnight braising or final seasoning. They see everything through a completely different lens. Experiencing the dishes through their perspective makes you more in tune with the customer journey.

Elements like background music (too loud, too quiet, wrong vibe), cleanliness, lighting, comfort, air conditioning can also impact the dining experience but may be beyond your direct control. These are best raised with the management team to enhance the overall offer.

It's entirely likely your customer has a very different range of subconscious thoughts running through their mind as they enter the venue...things like:

- What do I feel like eating today?
- How did the staff make me feel upon arrival?
- Once ordered, how long did it take for the food to arrive?
- Was the room too noisy, too lively, or too hectic for my occasion?
- Did the food meet my expectations based on the menu description?
- Was the overall experience worth the price?
- Was I happy to leave a tip when it came time to pay?
- Would I return for this experience again?

Secret Sauce

And that's just the tip of the iceberg. There's so much emotional energy involved in hospitality. In some cases, customers get more upset over a cold cup of coffee than they do over a major purchase like a new car!

While you can't cover every aspect, it's important to walk in the customer's shoes every now and again.

Key Chapter Takeaways

The customer journey

The experience your guests have from booking to the final bite is the key to your restaurant's success. It's not just about what happens in the kitchen – it's every interaction, from the first online click to the overall ambience, the staff's professionalism, and even the cleanliness of the facilities. A memorable customer journey is essential in shaping your restaurant's identity.

Clarity and consistency

You need to be clear about your story and the experience you want to deliver. Consistency across all touchpoints – menu, staff, atmosphere – ensures that customers know exactly what to expect, building trust and loyalty.

Align your vision

Your food philosophy isn't just an idea – it should align with your market and your business identity. Understand what works for your local community, your team and your customers. This alignment between what you want to achieve and what your customers need leads to long-term success.

Your Mise en Place

Complete these tasks to get the most out of this chapter...

➢ **Define your philosophy**
Take time to craft or clarify your food philosophy and ensure it aligns with the business's identity. This is the foundation of your kitchen leadership and will shape every decision, from menu planning to customer interaction.

➢ **Understand your customer**
Analyse your menu sales and customer reviews to ensure your offerings meet expectations. Profile the perfect customer and pre-empt their wants and needs. Add Will Guidara's *'Unreasonable Hospitality'* to your reading list.

➢ **Walk in the customer's shoes**
Approach your venue with fresh eyes, seeing every touchpoint from their perspective. Write down what is done well, what could be smoother and identify any gaps in the journey that can be worked through to create a memorable experience at every stage.

Chapter 5

The Ecosystem

Purchasing

"Relationships are pivotal to the success and wellbeing of any business. We care for the customer, care for the staff and care for the suppliers."

- Neil Perry

By now, you're getting a clear sense of your positioning in the market – how the business views itself, what your customers expect, and how your operation fits into the local community. This understanding is crucial when it comes to shaping your purchasing strategy.

You've probably heard the saying, 'It takes a village to raise a child'. Well, the same idea applies to a hospitality business.

Restaurants are delicate ecosystems, deeply interconnected and dependent on constant collaboration. Suppliers, farmers, fishermen and producers aren't just vendors — they're part of your extended family. These passionate individuals work tirelessly to provide the quality ingredients you rely on to craft memorable dishes.

When it comes to supplier relationships, a trusted business mentor once shared an invaluable lesson: "Always leave something on the table for someone else". Sure, you could drive a hard bargain, but squeezing suppliers too much only shifts the burden onto them. If they falter or go out of business, your supply chain crumbles. A smarter approach is to focus on value. Quality comes at a cost, and if your customers aren't willing to pay for premium meals, then perhaps your purchasing and positioning are out of sync, and need to be reviewed.

Here's the reality: buying cheap often means your team will have to work twice as hard to make a subpar product shine. You can put lipstick on a pig, but it's still a pig. As a kitchen leader, it's your job to balance quality, cost, and fit-for-purpose ingredients to keep the ecosystem thriving and deliver on your customer promise.

Relationships

The supply chain is the lifeblood of your restaurant, bringing immense value to your operation. From the grower, the delivery driver to the sales rep, each person in the chain has unique insights to offer — if you take the time to build relationships with them. Because they move between sites and interact with a wide variety of businesses, they're invaluable for keeping your finger on the pulse of the industry. These are the people who know what's trending, what's coming to market, how seasons are shaping up, and even what's happening at other competitor venues.

But, like any relationship, it's a two-way street. Small gestures can make a big difference. For example, I always made it a habit to prepare a takeaway coffee for the seafood delivery driver during those early morning drops. It was a minor effort on my part but immensely appreciated by the driver – and it paid off. Our venue became their top priority, ensuring we always received our deliveries first when schedules were tight or things went wrong. Little acts of goodwill build trust and synergy, creating partnerships that truly work for you.

Suppliers also love seeing their products shine. Industry events and competitions, like the Nestlé Golden Chef's Hat, showcase young chefs' talent while demonstrating creative use of sponsored ingredients. Suppliers are thrilled when their products are used in innovative ways. It's not just about the sale; it's about the story and the collaboration. Competitions don't always need to be of a huge scale, just using this concept in a staff meal promotes engagement with your team, and gets the suppliers involved.

Your sales reps want to see you succeed because your success moves their product. Leverage their expertise – ask them what's working in other venues, and what promotions or partnerships could support your goals. Think beyond the basics: sponsorship for theme nights, farm visits, factory tours, apprentice competitions and industry events. These collaborations strengthen the ecosystem and ensure mutual benefits.

And let's not forget about equipment and essential services. Equipment is a huge investment, and reliability is non-negotiable. The last thing you want is your oven breaking down mid-service, only to discover the replacement part is a week away. Cheap options may save you upfront, but the long-term costs of breakdowns, delays and inefficiency can cripple your operation.

When equipment fails, labour costs go up – plain and simple. That's why building a reliable network of repair professionals, spare parts suppliers, plumbers, electricians, and trusted service providers is critical. These are the people who'll save the day when things go sideways. It's not always about finding the cheapest quote; it's about knowing who will deliver when the stakes are high.

While some of the relationships and contacts you develop now might be at a base level, as you grow in your career, so do they. In the years ahead, the people you have supported get promoted into key roles including business development, head of sales or general manager. Some of the connections I made years ago are still friends and colleagues 25 years later! Start building your network now, and you'll find the good ones always keep in touch and are there when you need. A strong network isn't just a resource – it's a cornerstone of long-term success.

Negotiation

This is an essential skill for chefs, whether it's working with suppliers, discussing team responsibilities, or even advocating for your own pay and benefits. It's not just about crunching numbers – it's about people. Strong interpersonal skills, like empathy and clear communication, can be just as important as understanding the financials.

Negotiation doesn't require you to be a cutthroat expert – it's about finding a balance where both parties benefit. When done right, negotiation helps both businesses grow together – a fair product for a fair market price. That said, fair doesn't mean naive. You shouldn't let yourself be taken advantage of, and the key to preventing that is preparation.

Know Your Market

Understand the landscape you're working in. Familiarise yourself with the options available and the typical pricing for your needs. A little research goes a long way in giving you confidence during discussions.

Just Ask

You'd be surprised how often just asking can yield results. Most negotiations come down to volume, so it's crucial to know your sales patterns and be able to forecast your usage. Before sitting down with a supplier, gather 12 months of data so you can speak confidently about your needs and projections.

A good conversation built on mutual respect will take you much further than any hardball tactics. As my dad used to say, "Never burn your bridges – but if you have to, make sure you blow them up!" Keep relationships intact where possible, but when something doesn't align with your values or needs, don't hesitate to walk away.

Here are a few steps to prepare for any negotiation:

1. **Define Your Goals:** Dream big! Ask yourself, "What's the ideal outcome for my kitchen?" Whether it's securing a better price, sourcing fresher ingredients, or improving delivery terms, know what you want to achieve.

2. **Have a Plan B:** Not every negotiation will go perfectly. Outline alternative outcomes that would still benefit your kitchen. For instance, if you can't get a discount, maybe faster delivery times or extended payment terms could work instead.

3. **Spot Weaknesses (and Strengths):** Consider what factors might affect the supplier's position. Are they competing for your business? Are they introducing a new product they want to promote? Use these insights to your advantage.

4. **Emphasise Mutual Benefits:** Negotiation works best when both parties win. Frame your proposal in a way that highlights how it helps the supplier too. For example, committing to larger orders or a long-term relationship might incentivise them to meet your terms.

5. **Take a Breath:** Don't feel pressured to make immediate decisions. If you need time to reflect, use a phrase like, 'Let me review this with my team and get back to you'. This gives you space to step back, remove emotion, and assess the deal objectively.

6. **Prepare Thoroughly:** Follow the rule of the 6 Ps: *'Prior Preparation Prevents Piss Poor Performance'*. Be ready with data, goals, and a clear plan. Walk into the meeting confident and informed – you'll be much harder to rattle.

Adapting Your Style
Every negotiation is different. Adjust your tone and approach depending on the context – whether it's a casual conversation with a supplier, a formal email exchange, or a high-stakes meeting with an employer. Finding your style takes practice, so don't worry if it feels awkward at first.

Finally, remember that not every deal will be the right fit. If a proposal doesn't align with your goals, step back respectfully to keep the door open for future opportunities. Burnt bridges are hard to rebuild, so leave things on good terms whenever possible – be professional, not abrasive.

Play the Long Game
It's easy, especially under pressure, to lash out at a supplier, make demands, or push for the impossible. But remember, they're doing their best too. If you push too hard or develop a reputation for being difficult, it can backfire. It's a small industry and suppliers always know when bad debts are

accumulating. If you're in this industry for the long haul, focus on building sustainable, respectful relationships. Your success is tied to theirs. Respect the farmer, respect the product, and the ecosystem thrives.

One of the most impactful lessons I've learned came from running an apprentice training program. Instead of starting with standard culinary techniques – like boiling, frying, or mashing potatoes – I thought it would be interesting to flip the narrative. I took the students straight to the source. We spent a day on the farm meeting the grower, learning about different types of potatoes, their seasonal cycle, as well as the planting, watering, weeding and harvesting processes.

Then I had the apprentices dig their own spuds, connecting with the earth and harvesting several kilos of fresh potatoes. It was like they'd discovered gold, such was the excitement! After washing and preparing the potatoes, we all sat down with the farmer's family and shared a meal.

The transformation and learning outcomes were incredible. Talking about the humble potato is one thing, but to be unearthing them with your hands is a whole different level. The apprentices developed a profound respect for the farmer's effort and connected deeply with the produce. They understood the care it takes to grow food and carried that respect back to the kitchen, eliminating waste, handling ingredients with care and using them as the grower intended.

Now imagine applying this mindset across your kitchen.

The Ecosystem

- Do you know who presses your olive oil?
- Have you asked who harvests your fresh herbs each day?
- Have you considered who gets up in the early hours of the morning to source the freshest fish from the market?

Visiting your producers, touring facilities and understanding their processes is an eye-opening experience. It builds relationships grounded in mutual respect and understanding. Over time, attending industry events and working with the same suppliers for 10, 15, or even 20 years creates partnerships that are rewarding and stable.

I've seen procurement managers chase every penny, treating suppliers with disdain and grinding them down relentlessly. While this approach might save some money short-term, it's not sustainable. A good kitchen leader understands the importance of balance. It's not about fighting with people every day – it's about fostering collaboration. Because you never know when you'll need someone to step up and help you out.

Heartbeat
At the heart of every successful kitchen is a thriving network of relationships built on trust, respect and collaboration. Whether it's the farmer who grows your produce, the butcher breaking down the carcass or the delivery driver, each piece of the puzzle is essential.

Sure, you'll face challenges – tight budgets, tough negotiations and the temptation to cut corners. But remember, the long game is where real success lies. Building sustainable relationships isn't just good for business; it's good for your team, your suppliers and the industry as a whole.

Take the time to know your people and their stories. When you understand the effort behind the ingredients and equipment in your kitchen, you'll gain a deeper appreciation for the work we all do.

A great chef isn't just a master of flavours – they're a steward of their ecosystem.

Treat your suppliers with the same respect you'd want for yourself and you'll create a ripple effect that elevates not just your kitchen but the entire community around it.

Key Chapter Takeaways

Build strong relationships

Relationships are the backbone of long-term success in the kitchen. Recognise that you can't do it all alone. Whether it's suppliers, growers, or service providers, cultivating mutual respect and trust creates a network that supports your growth.

Hone your negotiation skills

Negotiation isn't about winning at someone else's expense; it's about achieving balanced outcomes that benefit both sides. Identify your current skill level, embrace discomfort in challenging conversations and actively practice and refine your approach.

Respect

Acknowledge the effort and energy that go into every part of the food supply chain. Show curiosity about what drives your suppliers and their businesses. Understanding their perspective deepens your collaboration and enhances the ecosystem.

Your Mise en Place

Complete these tasks to get the most out of this chapter...

➢ **Assess your negotiation skills**
Rate your negotiation skills on a scale of 1-10. Be honest with yourself – this isn't about perfection, but growth. What steps will you practice to increase this score?

➢ **Phone a friend**
Reach out to two people you consider skilled negotiators. Ask them how they approach negotiations, what strategies work for them, and any pitfalls to avoid. Apply their insights to your own practice.

➢ **Strengthen supplier relationships**
Identify your top three suppliers by dollar volume. Reflect on how you can enhance or maintain these partnerships over the next 3 to 5 years. Shifting to a long-term mindset transforms the conversation and helps you build more meaningful connections.

➢ **Map your ecosystem**
Create a visual representation of your kitchen relationships – whether it's a mind map, spreadsheet, or a quick sketch. Document

The Ecosystem

key suppliers, contacts, and connections. This exercise not only organises your network but also highlights gaps or opportunities you may have overlooked. As your career evolves, this map will grow with you, helping you maintain connections and stay anchored in a thriving network.

Chapter 6

Making Dough

Profit

"Know which side your bread is buttered."
- Proverb

Money Mindset

Let's start with this statement: there's nothing wrong with making money. The trade course apprentice chefs undertake is Certificate III in Commercial Cookery. Money has everything to do with the *commercial* part of this course.

As a kitchen leader, your money mindset isn't just a personal matter – it's foundational. Why? Because cash flow is the oxygen of your business. Without it, your team, suppliers, customers and future earning capability will suffer.

Secret Sauce

One of the biggest challenges when learning your cookery trade is that the theoretical component of making money through selling food is only briefly discussed during studies, when a young chef is usually not involved with ordering, designing menus or costing dishes. So, while the course provides a basic theory of how to cost a dish, there is minimal practical application, and therefore no context. This is like going to the gym one time with a personal trainer and calling yourself a bodybuilder. You're out of your league.

I knew a chef who was working in a large kitchen brigade of over 20 people. One day, the head chef decided to leave, taking the sous chef along with him to open a brand new multi-outlet boutique hotel. My friend, who knew the menu inside and out, could handle himself on a busy service and was well-respected within the team, found himself as the 'last man standing' and was asked by management to step into the head chef position.

Excited by the prospect of promotion, enticed by the lure of more money and challenged by increased responsibility, he accepted the role. For the first few weeks (the honeymoon period), all was well. Supportive comments from management, the team were engaged with the new leadership, the owners were happy as they didn't have to look externally and promoted from within. It seemed like a win-win.

Until the following month's P&L sheet landed. The head chef was called into a management meeting to explain the poor result. There was a whole different vibe from the positive encounters over the prior month. It felt hostile.

Making Dough

He was now accountable for the financial performance of the kitchen operations. Fingers were being pointed, questions were being raised – why is the labour so high? Why is the food cost up? Who is this new supplier you've brought on? Why are they demanding Cash on Delivery? Why do we have so many casual staff? Can you explain the amount of stock in the freezer?

Other questions were being raised about the predecessor. Scrambling to keep up with the pace of the meeting, the final words that struck with him were "You're the head chef now, you should know the answers – that's what we pay you for".

Leaving the meeting the chef was deflated. Within a few weeks he had resigned, taking some time off to plan the next step in his career. Not the way he'd hoped to complete three years with this employer. He left his work 'family' and friends, feeling like a failure.

This is not an uncommon story. Especially during a chef shortage.

This chapter explores the financial literacy required to run a kitchen. It explores the terminology, who to ask for support and the knowledge you need to make money from food and run a commercially viable kitchen.

Cash Flow
Cash flow isn't just a line on a spreadsheet – it's the oxygen of the business. Without consistent cash flow, even the most beloved restaurant will face financial suffocation. According

to industry statistics, 60% of restaurants struggle in their first year, and 80% fail within five years. Why? Cash flow issues.

Understanding cash flow means knowing where your money comes from, where it goes, and how to keep it circulating. Think of it like keeping a kitchen organised – you need the right tools, processes and timing to ensure success.

Depending on the era you grew up in, your mindset about money might have been shaped by growing up hearing comments like "Money doesn't grow on trees," "Don't be greedy," "Don't be so tight" or "Money is the root of all evil". These nuggets of wisdom can profoundly influence our habits and beliefs about finances.

This chapter isn't about turning you into a financial wizard, but it will challenge you to understand the basics and build a positive relationship with money. As Morgan Housel wrote in *The Psychology of Money*, "Money's greatest intrinsic value is the ability to give you control over your time".

What would that mean for you in your role?

- **Control over pressure**
- **Control over purchasing**
- **Control over profit**

Traditionally, there has placed little emphasis on the financial side of running a kitchen. At culinary training organisations, financial literacy is such a small module, leaving many chefs ill-prepared for the realities of understanding profit and loss (P&L) sheets. This gap in knowledge becomes glaringly apparent when chefs step into leadership roles where financial decisions make or break the business.

You don't know what you don't know.

With a clear, positive money mindset and a focus on cash flow, you can ask the right questions, know which levers to pull, challenge the data, have the right level of conversation and set the kitchen on a path to success.

Cash is king – but knowledge is power.

Let that concept guide you as we dive in.

Right Tool for the Right Job

Stepping into leadership roles, it's not about how fast you are during mise en place, how good your sense of seasoning is or how efficiently you can run the pans section. Kitchen admin and management will consume your valuable hours and focus.

Your job isn't to become an accountant; it's to ask the right questions, interpret the answers, and make informed decisions. It's your responsibility to understand the financial basics and be well informed. Relying on a sous chef or team member to handle the ordering and stock control when taking over a kitchen is risky – they may have been part of the original problem. With the right tools and mindset, you can transform financial literacy into a core strength of your kitchen leadership.

Today's modern kitchens have access to advanced technology, data insights, and specialised tools that can bridge this gap. From POS systems that track real-time sales data to inventory management apps that streamline stock control, the right tools empower chefs to make informed decisions quickly and efficiently.

Know Your Figures

What is a P&L? A profit and loss statement is a financial report that shows the business revenue, expenses and net profit (or loss) over a defined period of time. It's usually a month, a quarter or a year.

In terms of financial performance – the P&L is the scorecard by which you are judged. It is what businesses pay accountants and bookkeepers to manage. It informs the business on how well it is tracking to budget and previous periods and helps identify opportunities for improvement.

All key financial indicators and the overall financial position of the business are identified in the P&L. Good owners and managers will take time to discuss the elements that each team member is accountable for. It's only through understanding the language around the P&L that you can meet your budgets and financial goals. To use a football analogy, it's hard to score a goal if you don't have goal posts.

You don't need to learn it all, but by increasing your financial literacy you will be able to understand which levers can be adjusted to influence kitchen profitability.

Here's a high-level glossary, using a monthly P&L example:

- Food cost – how much you actually spend in a month on purchasing food from suppliers.
- Labour cost – the combined dollar figure for full-time salaries and casual wages paid to the team during the month.
- Overheads – fixed costs including rent, electricity, gas, sewerage, waste removal.
- Consumables – items that are not food, but related to preparing or selling food (think cling film, foil, gloves, disposable containers). Typically, these are not counted during stocktake, with the cost allocated at the time of purchase.
- Equipment – the stuff that you cook on, ovens, stoves, fryers, benches. This is a little unique from an accounting perspective because it is considered an asset, e.g. you can sell it if needed, therefore it is reported on in a different area.
- R&M – Repairs and Maintenance – the cost of parts plus labour to keep your kitchen operational (broken ovens, components for dishwashers, replacement thermostats for example).
- COGs – Cost of Goods Sold – this incorporates food cost and consumables and is the sum of all direct costs associated with making a dish.
- ROI – Return on Investment – the measurement of profitability relative to the initial investment. This is usually calculated as a percentage.
- Budget – what the business has forecasted you should spend / sell to achieve financial targets.

This is based on historical data with an increase to cover rising costs and inflation.
- CPI – Consumer Price Index – a measure of the average change over time in price for a basket of goods and services, commonly used to track inflation. Includes food, clothing, housing, insurance.
- GST – Good and Services Tax – this is the government tax on most goods and services.

Other terms worth mentioning:

- EBITA – Earnings Before Income Tax and Amortisation. This is a measure of a company's profitability that excludes interest and tax expenses, providing a clearer picture of its operational performance.
- GP – Gross Profit – the difference in value between the selling price of a dish and the cost of ingredients and materials used to make it. As a formula:

> **GROSS PROFIT = TOTAL SALES REVENUE – COST OF GOODS SOLD**

As a percentage:

> **GROSS PROFIT MARGIN = (GROSS PROFIT / TOTAL SALES REVENUE) x 100**

Why it Matters?

Gross profit is your financial health. It lets you know how much you have left to spend, and does not factor in operating expenses like overheads, labour, equipment and repairs. It's like a report card for your efficiency but does not directly translate to being profitable. By keeping an eye on the gross profit regularly, you'll be in a much better position to make smart, informed decisions that impact your kitchen's bottom line such as menu pricing.

- Net profit – your net profit is the amount leftover from the gross profit after you deduct operating expenses. As a formula:

> **NET PROFIT = GROSS PROFIT – (OPERATING EXPENSES and TAX)**

Net profit as a percentage:

> **(NET PROFIT / REVENUE) X 100**

As a kitchen leader you have direct influence in two important financial areas: COGs and labour.

Cost Of Goods Sold (COGs)

The cost of goods sold is an accounting term for the direct cost of producing the goods that a business sells. For kitchens, it measures the cost associated with producing each item on the menu. This typically means ingredients, consumables and packaging. Lower COGS means a better bottom line. High COGS means you are working hard to make less return.

Here are ten tips to effectively manage and reduce COGS:

1. Manage Stock Levels
Regularly check stock on hand to avoid over-ordering or shortages. Use the **FIFO (first in first out)** method to reduce waste and rotate fresh food. Holding too much inventory is unnecessary.

2. Minimise Waste
Train your team on portion control and creative ways to use leftovers. Track daily waste to identify and fix problem areas.

3. Optimise Your Menu
Focus on high-profit dishes with affordable ingredients. Review and update your menu regularly to remove costly or underperforming items. While you might love a 'signature dish' – let the data decide if it stays or gets replaced.

4. Build Supplier Relationships
Negotiate better prices by building strong relationships and understanding their business. Can you reduce frequency of delivery? Increase minimum spend? Consider bulk buying frequently used items. The more efficient you are as a customer, the sharper their pricing can be for you. Their knowledge of the market can be invaluable.

5. Standardise Recipes and Portions
Use precise recipes to ensure consistency and avoid over-portioning. Equip your team with tools like scales to maintain accuracy and be accountable to the correctly costed dishes. Small costs add up over a year.

6. Monitor Food Costs Regularly
Calculate food costs weekly or monthly to spot trends early. Use this data to adjust pricing or swap out expensive ingredients.

7. Prevent Theft
Limit access to storage areas and conduct regular audits on high value items against the stock movement. Have a set menu for staff meals and ensure a docket is run through for transparency.

8. Train and Motivate Your Team
Teach your team how their actions impact costs and profitability. Set expectations and reward them for meeting waste reduction or cost-saving goals.

9. Use Seasonal and Local Ingredients
Seasonal produce is often cheaper and fresher because it's in abundance. Local sourcing reduces transportation costs and supports the ecosystem.

10. Adjust Pricing Strategically
Regularly review menu prices to reflect current ingredient costs and CPI. Offer premium specials to balance out lower-margin items.

Kitchen Labour
This is the total cost of all the people who help bring your food to life each week. It's not just chefs and cooks – it also includes kitchen hands, storeroom staff, cleaning contractors, and even management. Essentially, it's everyone who plays a part in keeping your kitchen running smoothly.

Here are ten tips to manage kitchen labour effectively:

1. Master Rostering and Scheduling
Get to know your rostering system inside and out. Explore tech and software solutions that can make this easier and start having conversations about how they can help streamline your planning. Bookings and daily revenue forecasts should give you an idea of how much labour you need to prepare and run service for the projected customers. Simple things like removing a kitchen hand on a Monday lunch and placing a bucket of soapy water in washup can save valuable dollars.

2. Use Historical Data for Planning
Look back at historical data to compare similar trading periods. It's a great way to plan smarter and avoid over or under-staffing. Good revenue tends to mask inefficiency. Challenge the way you operate and avoid the temptation to copy and paste rosters. Failing to plan is planning to fail.

3. Put the Right People in the Right Roles
Make sure your most skilled team members are where they're needed most. For example, don't put a newbie on the grill during a busy Saturday night rush. This can lead to unnecessary wastage.

4. Coach and Train Your Team
Set clear expectations, give regular feedback and training. Your team can't improve if they don't know where they need to focus and how their actions contribute to the overall result.

5. Balanced Downtime
Make sure your team gets proper rest between shifts. Overwork leads to reduced efficiency, fatigue, illness or even burnout, which is costly for everyone.

6. Simplify Prep Work
Look for ways to reduce prep time, like batching tasks, overnight cooking or a dedicated preparation shift. Every minute saved adds up.

7. Know the Rules
Stay on top of awards and legislation to ensure you're paying your team correctly.

8. Be Transparent
Talk openly with your team about labour costs. When they understand how their work impacts the business, they're more likely to contribute positively.

9. Focus on Retention and Succession
Play the long game by investing in staff retention and planning for the future. A stable, skilled team is your key to success.

10. Kitchen Layout
This can get expensive but is worth mentioning. A well-designed kitchen where workstations are logically placed and equipment is easily accessible improves workflow. A few micro-movements like bending down to access a fridge, or steps to the cool room add up over the course of a year. A clutter-free, efficient setup helps your team work smarter, not harder.

Just like learning how to prepare and cook a new dish, first you've got to understand the ingredients, the method and expected result. When increasing your financial literacy about COGS and labour controls ask questions from those with expertise.

This may include the accountant, financial controller, business owner, mentor or manager. Seek advice to help you understand the P&L in the context of the business you are working in. Tap into their knowledge and experience, which is usually built on past wins and losses. Immerse yourself in meetings where possible, to gain experience and familiarise yourself with the terms and language.

The 80/20 Rule

Most of us want to achieve more with less. In the business classic *The 80/20 Principle: The Secret to Achieving More with Less* author Richard Koch demonstrates that a small number of causes (about 20%) often drive the majority (roughly 80%) of outcomes.

During this chapter we have covered a fair amount of financial detail and terminology. This section provides ideas on how to leverage that knowledge through applying the 80/20 rule.

This rule offers a powerful tool for focusing efforts on the actions you can take to impact kitchen profitability. Here are a few examples for applying the 80/20 rule to your kitchen data:

Top Sellers

20% of your menu items most likely account for 80% of the volume of food sales. Identify these top-selling items. These are the ones that will impact the overall cashflow. Check the standard recipes, portion size and ensure they are the heroes of the menu. Don't rush to change them, until you understand how it might impact your bottom line and why the customers order them.

Is it the price point or perception of value?
Is it a comfort food?
Is it a potential signature dish as voted by the customers?

Streamline these core items. Ensure you know the costs, margin and the team are following the correct process. You might be able to increase the sale price slightly to offset more expensive menu items.

Spend Per Head

20% of your customers are responsible for 80% of your revenue. This might be because of large tables, special events, additional courses or drinks. Identifying these loyal patrons and focusing on their experience can lead to more frequent visits and word-of-mouth referrals. If you know their needs, you can consider how to attract more like-minded customers and refine the food offer to reflect.

Purchasing

When you analyse purchasing data, you'll often find that about 20% of your ingredients account for 80% of your food cost. These will be the high-volume items — in other words, the ones you use the most. If you are a seafood restaurant, for example, then your volume of expenses will be on fresh fish, squid, prawns, and scallops.

Conduct a regular stocktake of your ingredient costs and ensure the highest-cost items such as your seafood, meats, or specialty items are properly stored, rotated and handled – as well as correctly portioned – to eliminate wastage.

Efficiency

The application of the rule also lends itself to efficiency. 20% of your staff might generate 80% of the production. These top performers should be nurtured, recognised and given opportunities to grow. By focusing on training and retaining this core group, you lay the foundations for productivity and consistency. Effective leadership often requires looking beyond immediate tasks to understand who on your team truly drives value.

Focus

This principle can also rely on your output and focus. If you dial in on the 20% of work that gives you the highest leverage points, then it's a great use of your time. Try not to major in the minor things. Busy does not equal effective.

Embracing the 80/20 rule in leadership isn't just about trimming excess or solving problems – it's a mindset shift that guides you to focus on what truly matters. By encouraging your team to identify patterns in their own work, you create a proactive, efficiency-focused culture.

Rise of the Machines

In the information age, data reigns supreme. The interpretation of data is even more powerful. Today, the smartphone acts as a portal to a vast universe of knowledge, placing the world's resources and insights at our fingertips. This digital revolution is reshaping every industry, and the culinary world is no exception. Attend any food trade show, and you'll notice an ever-growing presence of tech innovators. These companies are designing cutting-edge tools to help kitchen leaders navigate the complexities of their roles, streamlining operations and driving success.

You don't need to be a financial guru or a software engineer to harness the power of technology. Instead, what you need is the willingness to embrace it and use it strategically. Start by tapping into the expertise of the people behind the tools.

For instance, reach out to the sales representative or support team for your Point-of-Sale (POS) system. Invite them for a coffee and ask them to walk you through the system's full capabilities. Many of these systems are underutilised simply because their potential isn't fully understood. By taking the time to learn, you can unlock features that simplify tasks like tracking sales trends, managing inventory, or optimising menu pricing. AI is progressing data interpretation and utilisation at a rapid pace. At a recent restaurant conference one of the tech panel members stated – "There is a tsunami of A.I. coming, so you just need to determine which side you want to be on!"

Kitchen Tech

Think of technology like a good quality chef's knife. You wouldn't use it to slice bread or to fillet a fish. The first step is understanding the tool – what it's designed for, how to use it properly and its limitations. Once you grasp these basics, you can begin to explore how it fits into your specific operation. Technology's true power lies in its adaptability. The same inventory management software might be able to assist a kitchen to reduce waste while also forecasting demand for high-margin dishes. Clean data in equals clean data out.

Examples of Technology in Action

Consider the possibilities:

- **Inventory Management Systems**: These tools track your stock in real-time, alerting you to shortages or overages and reducing costly waste. They can even integrate with supplier platforms to streamline ordering.
- **Data Analytics in POS Systems**: Advanced POS systems offer more than just transaction tracking. They provide insights into peak hours, bestselling dishes, and underperforming menu items. Armed with this data, you can make informed decisions about staffing, promotions, or seasonal adjustments.
- **Labour Scheduling Software**: Analyse past patterns to optimise rostering, ensuring you're neither overstaffed nor stretched too thin. Busy trading days warrant having a bigger team.

Building Your Digital Network

Technology isn't just about hardware and software – it's also about leveraging your network. Engage with vendors, peers, and industry forums to stay updated on trends and innovations. Some of the best solutions come from shared experiences within the community. You don't need to be an expert, but you do need to know how to ask the right questions.

From Knowledge to Action

Embracing technology begins with a mindset shift. It's not a replacement for your expertise but an extension of it. A POS system won't make decisions for you, but it will give you the information you need to make smarter, faster choices. Take the time to learn, experiment, and refine how you use these tools.

Ultimately, technology is a partner in your success. Start small – pick one tool or system to focus on this month. Dive deep into its features and explore its potential to elevate your kitchen. As with any great recipe, the magic lies in understanding your ingredients and applying them with purpose.

Key Chapter Takeaways

Cash is king but knowledge is power

If you're leading a kitchen, understanding the financial side isn't optional – it's your secret weapon. Whether it's reading a P&L statement or knowing how to manage cash flow, this knowledge can make or break your operation. Too many chefs are thrown into leadership roles without proper training in these areas, and it shows when the pressure is on.

Focus on the 20%

Following the 80/20 rule is about working smarter, not harder. In your kitchen, a handful of dishes, ingredients, and even team members are responsible for the bulk of your success. Leverage your time and energy there initially for the biggest return.

Embrace the tech

Tools like POS systems and inventory management apps aren't just fancy gadgets – they're your allies. These systems can help you track sales, cut waste, and even predict trends, giving you the upper hand in running a smooth and profitable operation.

Your Mise en Place

Complete these tasks to get the most out of this chapter...

➢ **Get comfortable being uncomfortable**
Sit down with your manager or accountant and dive into the P&L statement. Learn what's driving your costs and how to rein them in. Pick one area to focus on – like labour or food costs – and start making small, measurable improvements.

➢ **Apply the 80/20 rule**
Find the dishes on your menu that bring in the most revenue and make sure they're costed properly. Take a look at your team. Who are your rockstars? Give them the tools, training and support they need to shine even brighter. Which suppliers are you spending the most money with? How strong is that relationship? Follow the data.

➢ **Know your tech**
Choose one tool – like your POS system – and learn its ins and outs. There's a good chance it's packed with features you're not even using yet. Use the data to make smarter decisions, like tweaking your roster for peak hours or highlighting your top-selling dishes. By taking

these steps, you'll not only run a better kitchen – you'll be building a stronger, more profitable business.

The Third Mastery

Safety

Chapter 7

Avoiding Burnout

Care

"The heat of the kitchen is not just about the temperature; it's about the pressure, the stress, the relentless pursuit of perfection. You either handle it, or it handles you."
   - Marco Pierre White

The Breakdown Comes Before the Breakthrough

You can't beat the adrenaline rush of executing a great service alongside your teammates. But like any drug it becomes addictive... always chasing the next rush with the next opportunity to maintain that creative flow and energy. Looking back over my career I can see the roller coaster of emotions that I've put myself through. Now the highs can be fantastic – learning new things, meeting new people, travelling and growing. But the lows can be super challenging – changing jobs, neglecting yourself, feeding your obsession, stress and ultimately...... burning out.

The old idea of 'work hard, play harder' doesn't really hold up anymore. I've heard so many people outside of hospitality talk about it as having 'antisocial hours,' but I think that's missing the point. Hospitality is one of the most social industries out there! It's fast-paced, exciting and always in demand – a place where everyone can find their groove. You get to have loads of fun while learning new skills, delivering amazing experiences and earning a living. Sure, it's nice to be on the other side of the bar enjoying a drink with friends, but there's nothing anti-social about being the one creating those moments. That's what hospitality is all about – crafting those unforgettable experiences for people to enjoy.

Part of the lure and the fun of the kitchen is a workplace that is really dynamic and goes through an energy shift every single day. There's the initial briefing, planning, mise en place, set up for service, slight pause then 'game time'. This flows into clean down, debrief, reset and getting ready to do it all again. It's never ever dull – and it never stops. It's a constant flow of energy.

As a kitchen leader, you are responsible for guiding the tempo, keeping your team on track, delivering to customer expectations, but more importantly not getting completely absorbed into the vortex. Knowing when and how to drop in and drop out of the constant flow of energy is important, because it's your role to not only support the day-to-day operations but to think ahead, plan contingencies and steer the ship. In other words, you need to work on the business, not in the business.

Crispy Wings

I had a colleague when I worked in the UK – probably one of the most capable chefs I have worked the stoves with. He was technically brilliant and his efficiency was second to none. We worked together for over a year, at a one Michelin-starred fine dining restaurant, which whet his appetite to progress. He subsequently progressed to a three Michelin-starred establishment, which was one of the top restaurants in the world. The quality of the experience and knowledge gained was exceptional on every level.

Now my friend had told me the pressure he was under to perform. As a chef de partie, he was accountable for the mise en place, the standards, wastage and every element freshly prepared each day. No exceptions. Zero margin for error. Although he had several commis chefs and apprentices working in the section, they were not yet able to prep at the required standards, so they were only entrusted to conduct menial tasks – picking herbs, washing lettuce, basic vegetable preparation. The full workload fell on him to ensure every single item was prepped, blanched, rolled or seasoned to perfection. Nothing less.

Over his time there the extensive hours, split shifts and sheer exhaustion took a toll. While he loved the learning, the calibre and the quality of it all – he was out of balance. We caught up for a beer during his tenure there and I commented on a really odd marking on his arm – like a tattoo. He laughed it off, stating it was nothing, just a light burn. In actual fact, he'd fallen asleep against the old-fashioned radiator (used for central heating in England) and did not wake up until hours later, with the scent of his own crispy skin in the air.

Put on Your Oxygen Mask First

Running a kitchen is a lot like being part of a flight crew during turbulence. You know the safety briefing – 'Put on your own oxygen mask before helping others'. It's the same in leadership. If you're running on fumes – exhausted, stressed, or stretched too thin – then you can't be there for your team when things heat up. Taking care of yourself first isn't selfish; it's what allows you to lead calmly and with clarity. Many organisations have identified that taking the time to invest in overall employee wellness leads to a happier, more productive workforce, with reduced sick leave and increased tenure. How would this translate to you and your kitchen team? Whether it's sitting down to a nutritional meal, replenishing energy through your favourite activity, or just taking a breather – when you're in good form your decision-making is better, no matter how chaotic the kitchen gets.

Wellness comes in two main aspects:

Physical – your energy levels, your output, diet, nutrition, hydration and exercise all contribute to this area. And like any form of exercise, the change doesn't happen immediately. It's not about perfection, it's about progress and making better choices. Sleep and recovery are just as important as diet and exercise, as they allow your body to recharge. The key is to discover what works best for you and stick with it.

It's the small daily habits done consistently over a period of time that yield long-lasting results.

Mental – a big shift in the corporate sector is around psychosocial safety, focusing on identifying, removing or minimising factors in the workplace that can have the potential to cause psychological harm. Stress is probably the biggest factor in this equation, and can manifest in different ways – in our bodies, our emotions, our behaviour. Stress can affect your sleep patterns and your appetite, and can include symptoms like headaches, skin irritation, migraines and peaks and troughs in your blood pressure.

Emotions impact our behaviour. Think of when you might wake up following a long workday and you're not in the right headspace – you need that first coffee as a kick start to get you going. You could even be a bit anxious, irritable, depressed or even angry. It's important to know that these emotions aren't just in your imagination – they might be signs of a biological reaction occurring in your mind and body due to accumulating stress. The good news is that there are simple things you can do every day and habits you can put in place to protect your health.

The Wellness Wheel
This tool was developed to help clients identify areas for personal growth and adopt a more balanced approach to

their careers. It offers a holistic perspective on well-being, highlighting the interconnectedness of key aspects of health and pinpointing opportunities for improvement. By addressing each component – such as connection, sleep, growth, diet, mindfulness and exercise – it ensures that no area of your well-being is overlooked. Bringing focus to the areas that are lacking for you leads to a better balance, better mental and physical health, a more sustainable lifestyle, and a reduced risk of burnout. Where focus goes, energy flows.

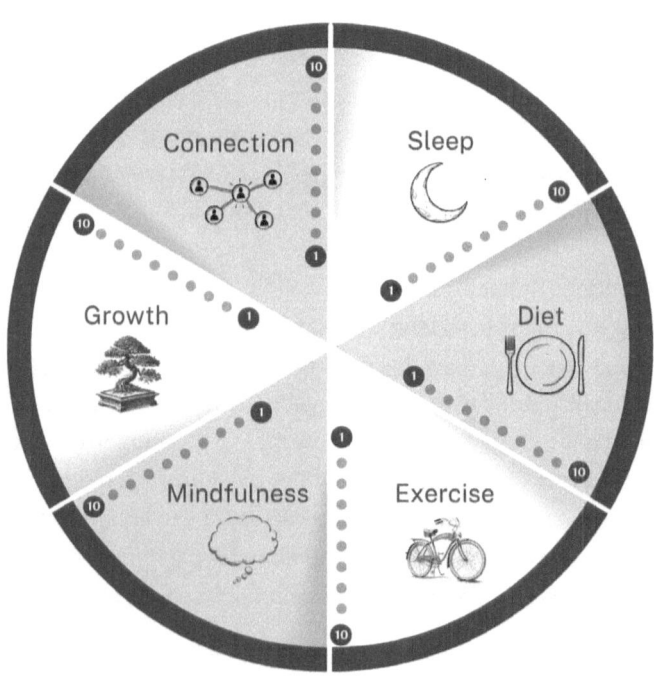

The Wellness Wheel

Sleep

A good night's sleep is so important for physical and mental recovery. What tends to happen as you get busier and step into a kitchen leadership role is that there's more 'thinking' and less 'doing'. This can lead to mental exhaustion and problem-solving late at night, when ideally you should be resting. Just like going to the gym, the recovery phase is as important as the exercise. One of the challenges, especially coming off the back of a dinner service, is establishing a sleep routine to regulate your inner clock. Corporate workers complete a normal day, then there is the commute, exercise, meal and wind-down process prior to sleep. Chefs need to compress this into a short-time frame. Unsolved challenges throughout the day are hard to put down. The mind doesn't like open loops and as a problem-solving muscle, will keep revisiting the problem until there's a solution presented. Too many chefs say that when they are not at work, they're thinking about work. This is amplified in an industry where everyone's got an opinion – food media; social media and customer reviews are flowing to your smartphone 24/7. Being mindful of these challenges and knowing how to give your brain a rest is super important.

Diet

Most chefs I know are pretty average when it comes to fueling their own bodies properly. They're so focused on putting others first – crafting dishes with the customer experience front of mind – that they forget to show the same care for themselves. If you're living on a diet of coffee, energy drinks and deep-fried chips, it's only a matter of time before it catches up with you.

Secret Sauce

Anyone serious about their health knows that a balanced diet rich in whole foods doesn't just fuel the body – it fuels the mind too. Eating plenty of fruits, vegetables, lean proteins and healthy fats has a lasting impact on your physical and mental well-being. Studies show that a nutrient-dense diet can improve focus, energy levels, and even mood, which is crucial in a high-pressure environment like a kitchen.

It's not about perfection; it's about making small, sustainable changes. Swap that energy drink for a smoothie, or trade fries for roasted veggies. Your body will thank you for it. After all, you can't pour from an empty cup.

Exercise
Regular physical activity boosts mood and reduces stress while improving cardiovascular health and endurance. Thirty minutes each day is recommended, but finding activities you enjoy makes it easier to stay consistent, while doing exercise with someone else keeps you fully accountable. Walking, running, or cycling are perfect to do either by yourself or in a group. Some people like the energy of the gym, or find joining in a team sport like basketball or soccer is what they need to maintain a regular habit. Find what works for you, start small then invest the time in yourself.

Playing team sport is a great social connection. It makes you feel good about yourself, gets your heart level up and releases dopamine into your system. Not only that, exercise breeds more energy – which is what any high-performance athlete will tell you. It's great seeing a mindset shift coming through hospitality operations, moving from after work drinks into after work boot camp.

When I was working overseas, we would work split shifts five days a week, a straight shift on Saturday and the restaurant was closed on Sunday. At first, during the split shift I'd go and rest, perhaps have a short nap because I felt tired. But I also realised I was just wasting a whole lot of time. I joined the local gym so instead of sleeping I was exercising. It was a contrast in tempo and momentum. I felt more alert, had more clarity, was eating better and had much more energy when getting back into the evening shift. Sure there was friction at first, but once the habit was in place, it was easy to maintain.

Considering the sheer physicality of the trade, 10 to 12 hour shifts at times, constantly lifting pots, slicing and dicing hundreds of times each shift – there is definitely a need to be match fit, if you want to prolong your career. Starting your day off with exercise is recommended, then it's out of the way and there is no room for afternoon excuses. Walk the dog, jump in the ocean, go for a run or work out. The key is to establish a daily habit, as the compound effect over a month or year is significant. If you can't, then be sure to close the day out with at least a brief walk to get the blood flowing and clear the head. Don't stress about it – there is always opportunity tomorrow.

Mindfulness

Practicing mindfulness is about building self-awareness and learning to manage your emotions, which can help you handle life's challenges with more resilience. Techniques like meditation and deep breathing are great for reducing anxiety and sharpening focus, but mindfulness doesn't always have to look like a formal session. It's really about being fully present in the moment, in a way that works for you.

Mindfulness doesn't have to be complicated – small, intentional moments will help you stay grounded. In Chapter 3 we referenced the concept of taking 4 seconds before reacting to a stressful situation. It's a simple trick, but it can make a big difference. Another easy practice is taking a short walk in nature, whether it's a park or even your backyard. Pay attention to your heartbeat, the sound of leaves rustling, the grass against your skin or the touch of a slight breeze. These small habits are surprisingly effective for managing stress.

Mindfulness also plays a big role in cooking. During my time with *MasterChef Australia*, I loved hearing contestants describe cooking as their happy place. When you strip away the chaos of a busy kitchen and focus on the craft – slicing, stirring, tasting – it becomes a powerful form of mindfulness. Cooking engages all your senses, making it creative, explorative and deeply satisfying. Plus, it's a way to nourish both others and yourself.

In the Netflix documentary *'Beckham'*, David Beckham shares how cooking helps him unwind. He has an immaculate kitchen on his estate and finds it incredibly relaxing, which is notable for someone with OCD who thrives on order. Cooking has the power to bring us into the moment and remind us why we love what we do. It's mindfulness at its finest.

Growth
Growth is about dedicating time to learning and developing in areas that matter to you. Studies show that pursuing personal development leads to happier, more successful, and fulfilling lives. Carol Dweck's book *Mindset* introduces the concept of a growth mindset – a powerful theory that highlights how shifting your mindset can influence the way you approach challenges, respond to criticism and set goals. Adopting a growth mindset helps you see obstacles as opportunities to learn rather than barriers, ultimately enhancing performance and enriching your overall life experience.

A philosophy I personally embrace is *kaizen*, a Japanese term meaning 'continuous improvement'. Making small, consistent changes to processes or behaviours improves efficiency and quality over time. While often applied in business, kaizen is just as powerful for personal growth, encouraging ongoing development and constantly striving to improve every part of your life.

Connection
Strong social connections are essential for emotional support and overall wellbeing. Spending quality time with others and maintaining open communication helps foster a sense of belonging. Engaging with a community can add meaning to your life and provide a greater sense of purpose. In his book *Tribes: We Need You to Lead Us*, author Seth Godin emphasises that humans have an innate need to belong. As a kitchen leader, it's crucial to have something you believe in and a team of like-minded individuals who will follow your

lead. Godin puts it simply: *"You can't have a tribe without a leader – and you can't be a leader without a tribe".*

Connection also extends to positive industry relationships, online communities, and maintaining supportive personal bonds (remember the *Eco-System* chapter?). Spending time with people who uplift and support you plays a key role in your growth. Motivational speaker Jim Rohn famously said, "You are the average of the five people you spend the most time with". The people you surround yourself with have a significant impact on who you become. If you're around motivated and positive people, they'll inspire you to reach new heights. But if your circle is made up of negative or complacent individuals, it can hold you back.

This is a good reminder to carefully choose who you surround yourself with on your leadership journey. Chefs love chatting with other chefs, so don't hesitate to pick up the phone, share your challenges and release some pressure regularly. Mentors play a big part here too – lean on them for fresh perspectives when you're feeling stuck.

Connect the Dots

Now that you've read through each of the wellness components, hopefully it's given you a clearer understanding of areas that are relevant to you. To conduct a simple self-audit using the Wellness Wheel, read the questions below and rate yourself a between 1 and 10 for each category using this scale:

Avoiding Burnout

Be honest with yourself about what you're doing well and where you're not doing so well.

Sleep: Are you getting enough high-quality deep sleep?

Diet: Are you getting the right level of nutrition?

Exercise: Are you engaging in 30-60 mins of physical activity each day?

Mindfulness: Are you actively engaging in mindful activities for 15 mins each day? Examples include yoga, meditation, deep breathing, reflection.

Growth: Are you learning and developing in areas that are important to you?

Connection: Are you maintaining supportive connections and relationships with family, friends and colleagues?

Map your score onto the Wellness Wheel and connect the dots.

- What feelings and thoughts arise through completing this activity?
- What areas have you identified that will re-balance your wheel?

- What simple actions can you take to shift your score?
- What will you commit to?

Neglecting areas of the Wellness Wheel is a fast track to burnout.

Sometimes, the breakdown happens before the breakthrough – but that's a choice. It's tough to watch, but even harder to experience.

Key Chapter Takeaways

The highs and lows of hospitality

The kitchen environment is dynamic, full of adrenaline and comes with significant emotional highs and lows. The buzz of great service can be addictive, but the burnout from long shifts, lack of self-care, and ignoring personal balance can take a heavy mental and physical toll.

Challenging cultural perceptions

The stigma of 'antisocial hours' in hospitality needs to be challenged. Working in hospitality is not just about long hours, but creating enjoyable experiences for customers. It's a social and creative environment that demands teamwork and constant energy, making it a unique and fulfilling career when approached with the right mindset. As a leader, you get to set the tempo for a positive environment. Be part of the solution.

Taking care of yourself first

It's essential to manage your own well-being before you can effectively lead your team. Prioritising self-care – through proper sleep, diet, exercise, and mental wellness – helps reduce stress, improves clarity, and enables better decision-making, ultimately benefiting both your personal life and your leadership ability.

Your Mise en Place

Complete these tasks to get the most out of this chapter...

➢ **Top Three Ideas**
Without overthinking it, write down your top 3 ideas from this chapter that you can put into action right now. Keep it simple – small steps create real momentum.

➢ **Do the work**
Complete the *Wellness Wheel* activity. There's no right or wrong – just be honest with yourself. Then, share your insights with someone you trust who can help keep you accountable.

➢ **Circle Back**
Set a calendar reminder for six months from now. Revisit the activity and reflect on what's shifted. What's improved? What still needs attention? *Where focus goes, energy flows.*

Chapter 8

Mise en Place

Compliance

"Mise en place is the religion of all good line cooks."

- Anthony Bourdain

Back of House

You can tell a lot about a chef by the state of their cool room.

It's not customer-facing – it's hidden away, out of sight. Yet it represents so much more in terms of systems, processes and habits, because the way you do one thing is an indicator of the way you do many things.

Secret Sauce

The benchmark of performance is how you behave and act when no one is watching. The cool room is a great indicator of the whole team's approach to hygiene, care for produce, stock rotation, sectional organisation, mise en place, stock control and freshness of produce. Think of it in terms of a mechanic's garage – would you rather have your brakes serviced by a mechanic who had all their tools organised, a tidy floor and safe, operational hoist, or from a mechanic with a cluttered workshop in disarray?

A very successful hospitality client I work with oversees a team of hundreds of staff across multiple venues. He's a hospitality operator through and through and we often have a laugh about how he always seems to find himself in the cool room of a venue having a conversation with the chef. The insights he gleans from such a conversation are impressive. Getting a feel of the heartbeat of the venue, just by simply meeting the person in charge of back of house operations.

In one of my strategic roles looking after over 300 venues I'd always start a kitchen health check by walking through the cool room. If the produce was handled with care, food covered, correctly labelled and rotated, there was no expired stock and most importantly it was clean – then I had a high level of confidence about the overall kitchen operations. In most cases, the financials were on target too. They seemed to go hand in hand.

It's important to remember that it's the back of house area that the customers would never see. It's a reflection of the quality and professionalism of the operation.

Mise en Place

An organised back of house indicates:
- Good hygiene practices
- Professional standards
- Staff are being taught good habits
- The chefs give a shit about the food they purchase

On top of this, the advantages include:
- Easier to clean and maintain
- Reduced risk of cross-contamination
- Easier to find the produce you need efficiently
- Reduced risk of over-ordering

As well as the commercial benefits:
- Reduced wastage
- Better stock control
- Streamlined stock take
- More efficient ordering

Running a clean back of house also sets the tone for an efficient and organised front of house. Good habits start with the baseline – they are what you do when you think no one else is looking. If there is no care taken to look after the produce you've just purchased, it usually equates to one of these things:

1. Lack of skill
2. Lack of standards
3. Lack of accountability

Having a compliant operation is a fundamental pillar in your kitchen leadership journey, and all of these three points are within your area of influence. Running a strong back of house operation allows you to focus on getting the standards right, the consistency right and ensuring things are done correctly day in day out. Chefs who run a poor back of house operation are exposed to risk and litigation. On an average day this can lead to bad customer reviews via social media which tarnishes the brand. On a really bad day – food poisoning or an anaphylactic reaction through mistreatment of food, which is far more serious.

A business owner or board member can be held personally liable if the business does not comply with food safety standards. It's their responsibility to exercise oversight of compliance and monitor food safety risks.

That's how serious it is. And as a kitchen leader you are 100% accountable. There's nowhere to hide when shit goes down.

Work Clean

In *Work Clean: The Life-Changing Power of Mise-En-Place to Organize Your Life, Work, and Mind*, author Dan Charnas takes the concept of mise en place – something every chef knows by heart – and shows how it can transform more than just a kitchen. By talking to top chefs including the likes of Thomas Keller, he digs into how this simple principle can help anyone get organised, stay focused, and get things done.

The magic of mise en place isn't just about lining up your ingredients; it's about having a system, a game plan that keeps the chaos under control and makes everything flow. It's about clarity: knowing what needs to happen, in what order, and who's responsible for each component, which sets the team up for success.

But mise en place isn't just about physical organisation. It's also about getting your head in the game. It's the calm before the storm, where you mentally prepare, prioritise what matters and ensure you're ready to lead. Charnas makes a great point: when you're focused on the right things and not distracted by the little stuff, you can lead with confidence – even when the pressure's on.

The big takeaway? Success in the kitchen – or anywhere – doesn't just happen during the busy moments. It happens in the preparation, in the systems you create and in how you set yourself and your team up for a win. So, if you're looking for a way to make your kitchen (and your life) run smoother, Charnas' insights are worth a read – and definitely worth trying out.

Systems and Checklists

Most chefs have a high degree of creativity, and it's this very trait that draws them towards the craft. But scaling the creativity and running a high-pressure kitchen environment is much more systemised than you might think. From a customer perspective, consistency is absolutely critical. They're looking to replicate the same feeling and emotion from an experience they had on a previous visit, whether that was last week or last year.

So how does the kitchen leader provide consistency through lunch and dinner seven days a week? Through great systems and checklists. Without the systems and checklists in place there is no standard to train to.

Take a standard recipe card. A recipe is a tool to provide a consistent, replicable result, time after time, year after year. Standard recipes provide units of measurement, ingredients, a sequence, a method and a reference image. All the best kitchens I've been in have these and usually a few little handwritten notes because they were always evolving and fine-tuning.

I know you already know this, because mise en place is one of the first cookery terms taught at TAFE or college. I'm encouraging you to take that term and instead of applying it directly to the preparation list for the day, think about the list for the whole kitchen and for your leadership journey.

- What systems do you already have in place?
- Are they being utilised?
- How can it be improved or refined?
- Can you engage your team to revise them so they're relevant and useful?

In Chapter 6 we spoke about the rise of technology and AI, which are perfect tools to leverage to ensure your compliance is on track and your systems are robust. Stress test your systems often to make sure they're still relevant. It's not about having rules for rules' sake, it's about having the right tools to support your team so the customer has a consistent experience when you're having a day off.

Mise en Place

I was running a catering company with a team of 20 staff and when promoted into the executive chef role, I realised that we had some very good systems in place. I wanted to train my team and empower them to run them. I'd identified three strong team members and invested time and energy in their development in key areas of the kitchen operation:

- Production and preparation
- Ordering and stock control
- Rostering and labour

After six months of ongoing training, the kitchen ran efficiently in my absence. It was a beautiful thing to see how fast the three chefs had grown and how responsible they were in each of their roles. It was no easy task for me to let go of complete control, but the fact of the matter was the kitchen was a lot more efficient. The upside was I became a lot less stressed. I'd check in with my chef who looked after labour first thing in the morning to see if I needed to assist any section or to troubleshoot. The usual response was, "No we've got this chef, you just do what you need to do". It gave me the capacity and ability to develop menus, train others, dive into the financials and keep the business moving forward. It allowed me to leverage my time more effectively – working on the business, not in the business.

Habits

Compliance is such an integral part of kitchen training.

Think back to when you were a first-year apprentice just starting your kitchen journey. Everything you're learning and observing in those first few months are what you believe to be the standards of that environment. You don't know what you don't know. So if you trained in well-systemised kitchens under capable chefs then you'll appreciate the quality of the foundational knowledge you have.

I'm sure you've also worked in some environments that lacked structure, systems and compliance checklists. Things fall apart really quickly – from basic cleaning, hygiene and storage to stock rotation and temperature checking – suddenly the consistency of the food is at the whim of the person cooking it at the time, meaning that it might be brilliant for certain days of the week and inconsistent for others. The direct translation of mise en place is 'everything in place', and you can see how not adhering to that principle is a risky way to run a kitchen.

As James Clear states in the bestseller *Atomic Habits,* "You don't rise to the level of your goals – you fall to the level of your systems".

I think the method of stir-frying provides the perfect analogy. Everything is cut, sliced, prepped and organised in advance and there's no movement away from the wok once it's been fired up.

It's fast, it's furious and it's loaded with flavour, but the mise en place is always completed first.

It's Not About You
Systems are the unsung heroes of an efficient kitchen operation. Cleaning checklists, manual handling procedures,

even down to a meeting structure all help to provide a safe environment for your team and yourself. Taking time to analyse the risks and working out where the gaps are is an essential skill for you as a leader. Systems create a clear benchmark to train to. It takes time, effort and energy to create good systems but once created, they can be used time and time again. This is a foundational pillar that you're accountable for.

I'm not saying you need to do all the work yourself, but you need to challenge the team and challenge the business on what's important, what's in place and what needs to be improved. Don't just put your head in the sand and say that you're too busy. No one wants to see a staff member go home with an injury because they weren't properly trained in a standard operating procedure. It's funny when I think about it because almost every element of the kitchen wants to do harm, from the meat-slicing machine to the knives, flames, hot oil from the deep fryer, steam from the oven, slippery floors – every aspect can attack you, so it's important to provide the right training so everyone knows how to conduct themselves safely and professionally and be compliant in the kitchen.

Key Chapter Takeaways

Systems define success

You don't rise to the level of your goals – you fall to the level of your systems. Read that again. A well-structured kitchen depends on robust systems and checklists to maintain consistency, efficiency, and safety.

Back of house standards

The state of your cool room is a direct indicator of your kitchen's organisational habits. From hygiene and stock rotation to food quality, a well-organised back of house sets the tone for the entire operation and influences the quality of customer-facing results. This includes the staff area. Get it tidy!

Mise en place mindset

Mise en place is more than a culinary principle – it's a mindset. Proper preparation, clear processes, and consistent execution are essential to running a successful kitchen. It ensures smooth operations and sets the standard for your team.

Your Mise en Place

Complete these tasks to get the most out of this chapter...

➢ **Evaluate and enhance systems**
Conduct a review of your current systems and checklists to ensure they're effective and relevant. The kitchen is a fluid work environment so involve your team in refining these systems for input and ownership.

➢ **Prioritise training and compliance**
Conduct ongoing training programs to ensure all staff understand and follow standard operating procedures. Don't make assumptions – ask questions. From hygiene practices to risk management, your role is to set the tempo to instil a training culture. Enforce clear processes for stock rotation, cleaning schedules, and food preparation to minimise risks and maintain quality.

➢ **Check your cool room**
Make back of house inspections a routine practice. What's happening in your cool room right now, this moment? Take a photo and start to analyse the good, the bad and the ugly. How does this translate across your kitchen operations? Remember, good habits are what occurs when the staff don't think anyone is watching.

Chapter 9

The Heartbeat

Culture

"A fish rots from the head down."
- Ancient proverb

This proverb might not be biologically accurate – as any chef knows, decomposition starts in the gut. But as a metaphor for leadership, it's spot on. Culture, standards, and behaviour all start at the top. If leadership slips, the whole team feels it. Strong leadership sets the tone, poor leadership erodes it from within.

As a kitchen leader, you are on show 24/7. Your team are unconsciously (and sometimes consciously) watching your every move, kind of like a child to a parent. Every slice of your knife, every pinch of seasoning, wipe of a plate, or backhanded comment is being observed. You are modelling the accepted behaviour for your team. The standard you walk past is the standard you accept.

Culture Kings

What exactly is kitchen culture and why does it matter? Culture is the invisible thread running through everything – how your team behaves, how they communicate, how they treat each other and how much pride they take in their work. But here's the challenge: culture isn't easy to measure. It's not like tracking food costs or labour hours. Instead, it shows up in the energy of your team, how they support each other during service, and your ability to guide them.

A poor kitchen culture doesn't just hurt morale; it burns people out, makes it harder to attract and keep good staff and leads to inconsistencies in your food. It's the fast track to high turnover, low productivity and a lot of headaches you just don't need. As a leader, you've got the power to shape a culture where your team not only survives, but thrives.

It is well known that Thomas Keller of French Laundry fame always greets his staff at the start of the day. He shakes their hands, looks them in the eyes and asks how they're doing. He's been at the absolute pinnacle of the craft for years and never lets the stress of running a business or personal pressure get in the way of those meaningful interactions.

The Heartbeat

Don't underestimate the simple gesture of greeting your team at the start of their shift and thanking them at the end of the day. It goes a long way in building strong rapport and a positive workplace culture. This effortless act is completely within your control.

When I led the MasterChef food team, the workload was enormous – driven by tight shooting deadlines, the show's high profile, and the producers' relentless creativity as they pushed boundaries to keep it in the top ratings slot on television. My core team and I thrived on each other's energy, working together to deliver massive results under pressure. The production team and judges were always drawn to the test kitchen because of the vibrant energy, connection and atmosphere we created. There was always something exciting happening – whether it was testing a recipe, an innovative idea or a new dish in the works. A busy kitchen radiates a unique, positive energy that makes it an inspiring place to work. That's the power of culture – it shapes the environment and leaves a lasting impact.

When you were starting out your cookery journey, you were probably more of a sponge, soaking up the culture around you without much say in shaping it. Now that you're stepping into a leadership role, you're shifting into the driver's seat. This is your chance to set the tone – to create the kind of kitchen you'd want to work in.

In this chapter, we'll unpack the key ingredients of a healthy kitchen culture. From open communication to mutual respect, you'll learn how to build an environment where people feel empowered, supported, and ready to bring their best every day. A thriving culture doesn't just happen by accident – it's something you actively create.

Here are the key factors that impact culture:

1. Teamwork

Kitchens are high-pressure environments where timing and precision are important factors. A positive culture encourages sections to support each other, to be clear on their roles and to communicate effectively. Good teamwork is essential for bringing all the elements of a dish together at the right temperature at the right time, for controlling the tempo over the pass during service, and to ultimately to create a quality experience for the customers.

2. Consistency

Chefs and kitchen staff who feel proud of their work tend to support and maintain high standards, leading to better quality and consistency, which equals happy customers. When team members think they know better, or don't respect the leadership, they tend to cut corners and do things their own way. This creates disharmony in the ranks, which leads to friction. When team members value the standards in place, maintaining the expectations around work ethic, hygiene and personal presentation, the quality of the food will be more consistent, leading to repeat customer visitation. Repeat customers are the bread and butter of your business.

3. Respect

A good kitchen culture respects all roles, from the dishwasher through to the head chef. The workspace should create a sense of belonging and a purpose for everyone there. When people feel valued, their contribution increases and the turnover of staff is reduced. This is especially important through peak trading when you consider a team can spend a lot of hours together in a small space. Respectful culture also helps to prevent toxic behaviour like harassment or abuse, making the kitchen a safer and more inclusive workspace. As I mentioned earlier in the book, the commercial kitchen environment is not for everyone. It's challenging. Inclusion is not about making one person feel comfortable at the detriment of the team. This is a fine line to walk when focusing on a positive culture. Your role is to get the best out of your team while achieving the business goals, as well as having tough and truthful conversations if someone is underperforming. One bad apple……

4. Creativity

In such a fluid and ever-changing environment, scenarios requiring creativity are presented every day. It's an amazing part of being a chef. Customer requests, dietary considerations, seasonal variation, menu changes, specials and late deliveries demand the kitchen team adapt when handling highly perishable products. A strong and positive kitchen culture encourages creative input allowing different perspectives to be voiced and heard. This future-proofs the kitchen when challenges arise, promoting a 'can-do' attitude. Creative pressure creates increased urgency and focus – correctly harnessed this can be highly motivating and push boundaries. It provides opportunity to test your team's capability in real time, learning and growing from their wins and losses.

5. Passion

When people enjoy where they work, they are more likely to invest in their own development and growth, pushing them to learn new skills and experiment with new recipes or techniques. This passion often translates into better dishes, innovation and memorable customer experiences. This opportunity for growth keeps the team engaged and passionate to perform at their best. Passion can be a double-edged sword for young chefs. On the one hand, they're working hard to enjoy the rush and adrenaline of the kitchen, constantly working to tight deadlines and trying to avoid making mistakes. On the other hand, some employers take advantage of this, pushing chefs to work more hours, skip breaks and expecting high performance. Chefs are people too. You've walked in their shoes. As a leader you can now determine how to ignite and fuel their passion in a more sustainable way.

What Does Good Look Like?

For most of us, it's hard to pinpoint what good culture looks like, but it is easy to identify (through experience) what poor kitchen culture feels like. You see, humans are hardwired with negative bias. What this means is it's so much easier to identify what they don't like and harder to articulate what they actually want.

The Heartbeat

For example, a customer can easily identify and comment about things they don't like about their dining experience. You may have heard comments including: too salty, too small, too cold, too much spice, music too loud, don't like the flavour, it's not what I expected, I waited too long, it's missing an ingredient, too soft, too crunchy and the list goes on. You only need to check social media to understand this 'negative bias'. Statistically most people will have a good experience and share it with one other person. A negative experience they will share with at least ten people. This is easily amplified on social media.

So, what does a positive culture actually look and feel like? Let's flip it around and start by thinking about what a poor culture looks like. A bad culture includes things like:

- Low energy – everyone just going through the motions.
- Silence, no banter, and zero camaraderie.
- Poor communication – people not talking or sharing ideas.
- A vibe of fear or walking on eggshells.
- Constant pressure and stress with no relief.
- Unrealistic workloads that feel impossible.
- No empathy for personal balance or life outside work.

Your goal is to create the opposite of that. Aim for an environment where:

- There's good energy – people are engaged and motivated.

- Communication is clear and open – no guesswork.
- Casual banter and conversation flow naturally.
- Expectations and boundaries are well-defined.
- Pressure is managed with proper training and support.
- Workloads are balanced and realistic.
- Personal balance is respected, and expectations are clear.

It's all about creating a space where people feel valued, supported, and energised to do their best work. That's the kind of culture that makes a real difference.

If you know what type of environment works for you, then incorporate this into your planning. Be conscious of the types of behaviour that contribute to a positive kitchen culture. Discuss this with the team and lead them to set up the foundations. Sporting teams can take years to build a winning culture, but it always starts with the right level of leadership conversation.

Swim in Your Own Lane

When you're enhancing, rebuilding, or resetting your kitchen culture, there's one crucial thing to keep in mind: the needs and expectations of the people you're trying to attract. Sure, you've got your own way of doing things, and that's important, but putting your people first – truly considering what they need – can make all the difference.

As Sir Richard Branson famously said: *"I have always believed that the way you treat your employees is the way they will treat your customers"*. This philosophy applies to everyone, front and back of house.

Traditionally, kitchen teams have been situated behind the scenes, managing the intense pressures of running the 'engine room' of a restaurant. But as the design concept of open kitchens took hold, chefs are now thrust into the spotlight, on show for their work and adding to the theatre of the dining experience. The top-ranking establishments in the world understand that success is a collaboration. A beautifully cooked meal means little if it isn't delivered in a timely and professional fashion. The front of house team bridges the gap between the kitchen and the guest, making the whole dining experience flow.

Front of house staff often need to be emotionally intuitive and quick on their feet – anticipating every guest's need while making it all look effortless. Meanwhile, back of house teams bring focus, creativity, and precision. Together, they create the ultimate dining experience.

You might be thinking, *"But we're not a fine dining restaurant"*. And that's exactly the point. It's not about striving for Michelin star standards... it's about understanding your customers' expectations and aligning the team's actions to deliver on that expectation.

> ***Culture influences behaviour.***
> ***Behaviour influences actions.***

Developing the right culture builds a foundation for a thriving, long-term business.

Keeping it Real
Being true to the type of business you are is essential. Whether you're running a cozy soup kitchen serving honest, nourishing food or a modern gastropub with bold, creative flavours, your culture needs to reflect your vision.

For example, if your focus is on wholesome, scratch-made dishes, you'll want to attract team members who also share that same love for nourishing others and take pride in the craft of simple, produce-driven cooking. When you're clear on that vision from day one, it streamlines everything – hiring the right people, training them effectively, and building a team that truly embodies your values.

And here's a critical lesson: don't try to be all things to all people. Too often, I've seen chefs and managers get excited by an impressive résumé and bend over backward to make room for a potential 'rock star', only to quickly realise it's not about the best individual, it's the best team that gets results. Know who you're trying to attract.

Staff Meal
A great kitchen culture is like your Nanna's casserole – a load of simple ingredients that, when combined the right way, create something special. Not everyone has to get along all the time. In fact, different perspectives and creative friction can make the work – and the food – better.

The Heartbeat

Food has this incredible power to unite people. It's something we all share, no matter our culture, religion, or background. Some of the most amazing moments I've experienced in kitchens have been sitting down with a team from all over the world, sharing a meal, and breaking bread.

I interviewed veteran chef and restaurateur Neil Perry at the National Restaurant Conference and the topic came up about staff meals. Neil shared that the 'family meal' is an integral part of his culture at Margaret in Sydney's Double Bay.

Both the entire back of house and front of house team eat together at around 5pm, even if there are customers still dining in the restaurant.

The menu is planned and produce purchased specifically for the meal, not a by-product of the kitchen. Junior staff are encouraged to create the dishes, as a chance to showcase their skill and nourish the team. They enjoy the dining room atmosphere.

This is a powerful idea from a world-class operator.

Sourdough

As a leader, you don't need to dictate outcomes or have all of the answers. Instead, think of it like cultivating a sourdough starter. The base ingredients adapt to the environment, taking on characteristics of the time, place and people involved. Yes, it needs care, feeding, and attention, but much of the 'fermentation' happens organically. The starter develops depth naturally over time.

Secret Sauce

The best kitchen cultures grow this way.

At the heart of this growth is a clear and inspiring vision. This isn't about a corporate statement or something written on a wall. It's about defining the kind of culture you want to create in your kitchen.

- What values do you want your team to embody?
- What kind of environment do you want to foster every day?
- A strong vision for your culture acts as a compass, helping everyone – yourself included – stay aligned with what matters most.

Is your kitchen culture one of creativity and experimentation? Or is it focused on precision, consistency, and teamwork?

Rene Redzepi, internationally recognised for his unique reinterpretation of 'New Nordic' cuisine, drives a culture of curiosity, time and place when planning then menus at Noma. This approach has been tested and refined over many years, especially when relocating the entire dining concept around the world to places including Sydney, Kyoto, London and Tulum.

Perhaps your culture emphasises providing life skills to those less fortunate, or nurturing relationships, both within the team and with the customers you serve. Whatever your vision, it should reflect the goals of the business and the people who make up your team.

The Heartbeat

The vision for culture doesn't have to be static or perfect. Like a sourdough starter, it evolves with time and input. The important thing is to have clarity about what you're aiming for. This clarity shapes how you approach everything from hiring and training to resolving conflicts and celebrating successes.

So, take a moment to reflect: what is your vision for an exceptional kitchen culture? What do you want your team to feel, believe, and strive for every time they step into the kitchen? When you answer these questions, you're laying the foundation for a culture that thrives and sustains itself over the long term.

Key Chapter Takeaways

Culture is the foundation of success

The kitchen culture you foster impacts every aspect of your team's energy, collaboration, and morale, ultimately shaping the customer experience. A thriving culture creates a productive, engaged, and innovative team.

A leader's behaviour sets the tone

As a leader, you're always on show. Your actions – big or small – model the behaviour and standards your team will follow. The standard you walk past becomes the standard you accept.

Vision shapes culture

A clear and inspiring vision creates alignment, giving your team a shared sense of purpose and direction. When the culture aligns with the values of the team and the business, it unlocks their potential.

Your Mise en Place

Complete these tasks to get the most out of this chapter...

➢ **Define your vision**
Reflect on the kind of culture you want to create. What words or phrases come to mind when you think about the best environment for you and your team to thrive? Use these to shape conversations with your team about shared values and goals.

➢ **Observe and assess**
Take a step back and objectively observe your team's current behaviour. What actions, attitudes, or habits do you see? What are the positive actions and which ones are holding the team back? Use these insights to start identifying opportunities for cultural improvement.

➢ **Start conversations**
Open the dialogue with your team about culture. Ask questions like, "What do you like about working here?" or "What do you think we could improve?" Most importantly, listen intently to the answers.

> **Lead by example**
> Model the behaviour you want to see in your team. Whether it's consistent communication, respect, or passion for excellence, embody these traits every day. Remember, actions speak louder than words.

The Fourth Mastery

Quality

Chapter 10

Umami

Creativity

"There is not a good or a bad cuisine, just the one you like the best."
- Ferran Adrià

Umami

In the world of gastronomy, umami is more than a taste; it's a catalyst of inspiration. When chefs create, they reach for the fifth taste – not just to enhance flavours, but to unlock the layers of creativity and depth that bring their dishes to life. Umami is the savoury note that rounds out a dish, elevating it to something greater than the sum of its parts. For chefs, this is the alchemy of the creative process, where imagination, intuition and technique converge to transform ingredients into art.

Secret Sauce

Great chefs possess an almost intuitive understanding of how flavours interact, balancing each element until that "aha" moment when everything clicks into place.

Like a painter selecting pigments to achieve the right hue, chefs use ingredients including seaweed, fish, concentrated sauces, mushrooms, tomatoes, miso and parmesan to impart an undertone of richness that resonates on the taste buds. In the same way, they rely on their senses and palate 'memory' to weave elements together, layering flavours to create something harmonious, unexpected and memorable. The umami is difficult to pinpoint, yet its absence is always felt.

This chapter highlights the importance of creativity in your kitchen leadership journey. It explores examples of world-class operators, and how they approach their creative pursuit so you too can determine the best formula for your 'secret sauce'.

During my time running the MasterChef test kitchen, the contestants were asked to prepare and serve a dish that inspired them. The producers and editing team did a masterful job to capture the essence of the contestants, drawing on childhood experiences, a time with family, or location that was etched in their memories – such is the power of a good meal. The opportunity for you, leading a kitchen team, is to have that impact for your customers every single service.

The ability to create a memory 'burn' for customers, to curate those surprise and delight moments as they celebrate birthdays, milestones or friendship is a privilege not everyone gets to enjoy as much as a hospitality worker. It's an underappreciated superpower often discounted.

This concept is captured brilliantly through the eyes of food critic Anton Ego in Pixar's hit movie – *Ratatouille*.

Even more than that, this same transformative power extends to shaping your team. A well-timed word of encouragement, a patient demonstration of proper technique, or the decision to entrust them with additional responsibility – these small but significant actions can fundamentally alter the trajectory of someone's career.

Now is the opportunity for you to be the mentor your team needs at a critical time in their training. You've experienced this on some level before. Perhaps it was when the chef showed you how to plate their signature dish for the first time, or that shift when you were handed control of the pass during peak service. These are the moments that linger – like umami on the palate – complex, profound, and impossible to forget. They're the experiences that transform a cook into a leader.

Think about a milestone moment in your career, where you were trusted or encouraged to step up.

Who believed in you?
What did they say?
How did you feel?
What did you learn?
How did that change you?

Words have power.

Masterstock

You can't force innovation and creativity – they need space and time to flourish. As a kitchen leader, your role is to cultivate an environment where creative ideas can percolate naturally. Creativity, like a Chinese masterstock, is a process of gradual transformation and enrichment.

A masterstock is a blend of ingredients that deepens and evolves with every use. Unlike a fresh broth made for a single meal, a masterstock grows richer over time, absorbing the essence of each ingredient it touches. Traditionally composed of soy sauce, rice wine, star anise, ginger, and other aromatics, it becomes a liquid memory, layered with the flavour of duck, pork belly and vegetables from meals past. Over months or even years, it transforms into something far greater than its original components.

But for this richness to thrive, fresh ingredients must be continuously added – new aromatics, spices and proteins that release their essence as they simmer. The stock's life depends on this balance of honouring its past while embracing the present. It's not just about preserving flavour; it's about nurturing growth. A masterstock tells a story, evolving with time into a pot of liquid history – a tapestry of flavours that honours tradition while inspiring the future. One of my favourite TV chefs as an apprentice was Martin Yan on *Yan Can Cook*. His talent with a cleaver was captivating. I love his ethos on stock – *"It's like a strong foundation. When you have the right foundation, everything tastes good."*

Seasons

Over the years, I've developed a deep passion for the art of bonsai, and now I care for about 30 trees, each at a different stage of development. My journey began in Melbourne when my brother and I attended a bonsai exhibition. To my surprise, the president of the local Bonsai Club – someone about our age – demonstrated shaping a tree in under an hour. Watching him transform that unassuming tree into a masterpiece was mesmerising. Inspired, I decided to attend the club's next meeting, eager to learn more.

That first night, I was equal parts nervous and excited. I brought along what I thought was a promising juniper tree, hoping for feedback on pruning, wiring, and perhaps some guidance to give it a more rustic, aged appearance. After introducing myself to the group, I soon found myself surrounded by four of the club's senior members – a true 'brains trust' of bonsai wisdom. They asked about the tree: how long I'd had it, what I envisioned for its future, and what I liked about its current shape.

For over an hour they discussed its potential among themselves, reflecting on its form and theorising about what it could become. Finally, I asked the inevitable: "What do you think?" One of the experienced members stepped forward, pointed to the branches, and said, "If you cut this middle branch here, you'll redirect the tree's energy to the lower branch. Then trim the tip of the tree here – in about 20 seasons, you'll have an amazing bonsai."

I was floored. Twenty years??? I hadn't fully appreciated just how long it can take to shape a quality bonsai. This art has forced me to slow down, embrace the long game and be patient. But in that moment, I could only respond with: "That's great, but what can I do in the next 20 minutes!?"

Since then, there have been times when I've worked too aggressively on my trees – pruning too much foliage, disrupting the delicate root ball, or bending branches too much. The result is always the same: stress. This inhibits the bonsai development for a season and in the worst case, kills the tree. I keep the dead structure of these once-beautiful trees as a reminder of the dangers of rushing the process.

Limited Palate

As a young chef learning their craft, it's easy to get swept up in the excitement of creating new menu items – the sheer array of ingredients, textures, cooking methods, sauces and garnishes feels limitless. But as a chef matures in experience and refines their palate, they come to realise that it's often what you *leave off* the plate that makes the biggest impact.

Less is more.

This philosophy becomes especially powerful when you take the time to truly understand the quality of the produce you're working with. Years ago, during a trip to Rome, I had one of the most sublime pizzas of my life. It was utterly simple: a thin, perfectly baked base topped with tomato sugo, fresh mozzarella, and a single sprig of basil. The simplicity allowed the exceptional quality of the ingredients to shine through – uncomplicated, harmonious and perfect.

Umami

This lesson in restraint reminded me of something my late father, Jim, taught me. He was a talented Australian landscape artist who primarily worked in oils, and he often spoke about the power of using a limited palette of colour. By restricting the range of colours on the canvas, the painting achieved a sense of flow and harmony, drawing the viewer into its story. Dad explained that when artists use too many colours, it becomes increasingly difficult to make them blend and complement one another. However, starting with just a few primary hues and layering variations upon them creates a stunning array of shades, all connected and cohesive.

This concept isn't new – masters like Vermeer, Rembrandt, and Picasso embraced it in their work. Whether on a canvas or a plate, the principle remains the same: simplicity and restraint creates space for true creativity to flourish.

The Rueben

In his book *'The Creative Act – A Way of Being'* record producer Rick Rubin says that often the most innovative ideas come from either those who master the rules to such a degree they can see past them, or from those who never learned them at all.

Rubin was instrumental in altering the direction of popular music, steering the members of the Beastie Boys away from their punk roots and into rap. The 1986 debut album 'Licence to Ill' was the first hip hop album to reach #1 on the charts, and did more than any other recording to introduce the hip hop genre to the masses. It was his creative philosophy and his unwavering commitment to authenticity that empowered the artist to express their true selves. Rubin has worked with some of the biggest names on the planet including Run-D.M.C., Red Hot Chilli Peppers, U2, Johnny Cash, Metallica, Weezer and Adele, among others.

Rubin's musings highlight the importance of the creative expression and pursuit for not just artists but for anyone. As one of the most influential music producers of our generation, the alchemy he uses in bringing together genres to produce something so fundamentally transformative creates a ripple in time and in some instances, redefines conventional thought.

Rubin implores the reader to cherish creative expression to truly find their individual voice. The book offers practical advice around changing context, changing environments, and understanding what time of day is most conducive to creation. Rubin challenges us to never settle for the status quo or conform to conventional function – it's such a great snapshot into the mind of a creative genius!

A parallel can be drawn in the culinary world to pioneering chefs like Ferran Adrià (*El Bulli, Spain*), whose legendary curiosity redefined modern cuisine. His 'deconstructed cuisine' took classics apart while preserving their essence. Dishes including 'Carrot and Coconut Air'; 'Golden Quail Egg' and 'Parmesan Spaghetti' were conceived through his philosophy of reinventing familiar dishes by altering their textures, forms and temperatures to transform the diner experience, leaving a *memorable impression*. Such was his dedication to innovation that even at its peak, El Bulli closed for six months each year for research and development.

Charlie Trotter (*Charlie Trotters, Chicago*) instilled a culture of creativity within his brigade by changing the degustation menu every day for its 25 years of operation, reportedly never repeating a dish. Visiting the restaurant and kitchens in 1999, I noticed no cool room storage – only glass fronted display fridges. The chef advised this was because the produce was received, prepared and served daily. All fridges were empty by the end of the shift. Chef Trotter used this rigorous discipline to set a creative standard.

His first cookbook showcased combinations and techniques ahead of their time. In the introduction Trotter wrote "As the leader, I take total responsibility for what is served at Charlie Trotters.....I encourage spontaneity and welcome contributions of each member of the team – together we can reach even higher."

Both of these chefs were not about chasing trends, they had the guts to set them. While Adrià redefined technique, Trotter mastered the art of creative endurance. Their accolades weren't won by playing safe, but from reflecting on their experience and forming a new perspective to find their own unique style.

Season with Generosity

To elevate your craft, you must first master your creative process – then protect it fiercely. In the frenetic energy of the kitchen, the rarest ingredient isn't technique or talent, but *time*: Time to read, to taste, to wander, to reflect.

Inspiration is everywhere in life – walking in nature, traveling to different countries, exploring other cultures. That's where your umami lives: in the space between what's familiar and what makes you lean forward.

Our greatest creative act as leaders isn't just what we plate — it's the people we nourish. A kitchen should be a place where mistakes turn into lessons and potential is unlocked.

Understanding your creative rhythm and encouraging your team to find theirs is a superpower. That's the stuff that sticks — the kind of mentorship that lingers long after service ends.

Key Chapter Takeaways

Depth in the creative process

Creativity and innovation need time and space to develop. Just like a masterstock that grows richer over time, true creativity blossoms through gradual transformation. As a leader, it's essential to cultivate an environment where ideas can mature naturally.

The power of restraint

In the creative process, less is more. Understanding the value of simplicity – doing a few things exceptionally well focuses your energy. Like a painter using a limited palette, simplicity creates harmony and enhances creativity.

Lingering flavour

Great leadership, like umami, isn't always noticed – until it's gone. The best chefs? They're continually investing in their people. A well timed challenge, constructive feedback or word of encouragement all lift confidence and have the power to alter career trajectory. They're the experiences that linger for the long term.

Your Mise en Place

**Complete these tasks to get the
most out of this chapter...**

➤ **Define your career milestones**
Identify 2 – 3 significant turning points in your career. This could be a promotion you received, a course that expanded your knowledge or a competition that pushed your comfort zone, for example.

For each milestone, ask:
Challenge: What made this difficult?
People: Who supported / challenged you?
Emotion: How did you feel before / during / after?
Action: What specific steps did you take to succeed?

Write these as dot points and craft a short story from your answers. This will help you reveal patterns in how you overcome obstacles and strengths you can learn from and leverage.

➤ **Create space for creativity**
Allow your creativity and your team's ideas to evolve. Don't rush the process; nurture growth by fostering an environment where

new ideas can flourish gradually. Cultivate time for reflection and exploration. Reflect on the ingredients that form your 'masterstock' as it simmers. What do you love, what can you leave, what new aromatics can be added to enhance it right now?

➢ **Support your team**
Providing authentic, positive feedback is not always easy. Write down the names of 5 of your work colleagues. Under each name, list 5 things they do well. This brings focus onto the positive behaviours you are observing, which you can then comment on when the time is right.

Chapter 11

Every Plate, Every Time

Consistency

"A chef is only as good as their last meal."
- Gordon Ramsay

Service!

From a customer's perspective, consistency is king when it comes to food. It's not enough to create a great dish once. Your kitchen's reputation hinges on the daily standards you uphold – especially when the A-Team isn't on shift. Those standards become the benchmark by which your establishment is judged.

In this chapter, you'll learn how to maintain high standards when you're not onsite and hold your team accountable for delivering a consistent dish every time.

Secret Sauce

As a kitchen leader, the pass is your last line of defence. It's where the most senior chef coordinates with the front of house, catches potential errors before they reach the customer, and ensures every plate meets the mark. Running the pass is like conducting a symphony, where ingredients, cooking techniques and teamwork converge at the perfect moment to create magic on the plate.

Most customers won't comprehend the ripple effects of sending a dish back to the kitchen. For them, it's simply that the dish didn't meet their expectations – which can often be subjective. However, for the kitchen, a returned plate can disrupt the flow of service, turning a smooth operation into chaos.

Regular clientele are the lifeblood of any food business. As discussed in Chapter 6, the 80/20 principle also applies here: your regulars make up a significant portion of your revenue. Consider a quintessential pub. A pub, or 'public house', is deeply rooted in the community, dating back to ancient Roman times when alehouses connected towns and served as welcoming spaces for all. Today's pubs offer tap beers, wines, spirits, food and entertainment to the local community. Most regulars live within a 5-kilometre radius, making it crucial to understand their needs. What dishes draw them in? What represents value? What level of service keeps them coming back?

Pubs are a social hub – a place where neighbours gather, milestones are celebrated, and good memories are made. They also provide entry-level employment opportunities in kitchens and front of house roles. Pub patrons are often deeply loyal, but that loyalty hinges on consistency. If standards slip, customers might start exploring other local options. Over time, losing loyal patrons can significantly impact your business.

For instance, imagine a customer who dines at your establishment for 10 years, only to switch to a competitor because of inconsistent quality. The lost revenue over such a span is staggering. That's why getting the basics right — and maintaining them — isn't just important; it's essential to your success.

Training
Lionel Sternberger is reputed to have invented the cheeseburger in 1924 at the age of 16. He was working as a fry cook at his father's sandwich shop in Pasadena, California, and experimentally dropped a slab of American cheese on a sizzling hamburger. I don't know about you, but for me the combination of grilled beef, brioche bun, cheese, ketchup, mustard and pickle is a wonderous combination.

With over 41,000 restaurants in more than 100 countries, McDonald's is one of the most efficient and consistent food operators on the planet, serving millions of burgers daily. Whether you love them or hate them, no matter where you are in the world, customers know exactly what to expect when stepping into the Golden Arches. From the taste of the food, core menu items, hygiene standards and speed of service — it's always the same.

Secret Sauce

This is the kind of consistency customers crave. No discussion of nutritional value or quality. Just no surprises.

What sets McDonald's apart are the systems, procedures and training programs in place, to enable 15-year-old kids to deliver a uniform experience, every time. Ray Kroc, who expanded the original McDonald's from a small California burger joint into a global empire, was captivated by the meticulous systems the McDonald brothers had developed. His ability to see the magic in their processes is what allowed the business to expand globally, while maintaining consistency.

When it comes to your kitchen, consistency isn't just about the food. It extends to every element. Take hygiene as an example. Consider the casual dishwasher who only works one or two shifts each week. Despite their limited hours, they play a pivotal role in maintaining the overall kitchen's hygiene standards, because they are the area of risk – the weakest link.

It's just a game of experience – they aren't as involved in the day-to-day operations and may not feel as invested as the rest of the team. They know that after the shift, they will not be back again for several days. It takes longer to gain the right level of experience due to the fact they only work a few hours each week. As a kitchen leader, it's your job to recognise this potential gap and build training systems that account for it. By understanding where your team's experience and commitment levels vary, you can structure your training to ensure there are no weak links.

Every Plate, Every Time

This is where a solid training program comes into play. Without it, you'll find yourself constantly putting out fires instead of working proactively. It's not enough to just manage the team; you need to provide them with clear processes and checklists so everything runs smoothly, even in your absence.

These are the essential processes and checklists to ensure standards are upheld:

- Standard recipe cards (including ingredients, measurements, and method)
- Photos of each dish (most chefs are highly visual)
- Recipe costings (with portion sizes, food costs, and margins)
- Mise en place lists for each section (prep guide with par levels)
- Ordering lists (for stocktaking and maintaining par levels)

If these are not in place, then build them. If they are established, review and improve them. It's impossible to hold anyone accountable for their work if there is no benchmark to go back to.

Delegation

Leaders who try to do it all often find themselves frustrated — both with their team and themselves. This relentless pursuit of control ultimately leads to burnout. If you're hesitant to entrust others with responsibilities in your kitchen, it's worth reflecting on what might be holding you back. Delegation isn't just about efficiency; it's about trust, empowerment and growth, for both you and your team. The first step? Learning the art of letting go.

Here are 3 things that hold leaders back:

Control
As a kitchen leader, wanting to oversee every detail is understandable – but it's unsustainable. Trying to be everywhere at once quickly becomes a bottleneck to your growth and effectiveness. Instead, focus on the big picture and allow those in your charge to take on more responsibility.

Trust
If you don't trust your team, they won't trust you. It's a two-way street. It might be time to reset the relationship. Start with small tasks, allow creative expression, provide clear expectations on outcomes but don't tell them exactly what to do. Instead explain the desired outcome and focus on the bigger picture. This requires patience and consistent communication. A short-term effort here will yield long-term rewards.

Ego
For chefs with an overinflated ego (we've all worked with someone like this!), it can feel like everything revolves around them. That's not leadership – it's dictatorship. While a healthy dose of confidence can energise and motivate, too much ego becomes a liability. A good friend and incredible chef I trained under, Paul Scott, once shared a thought that stuck with me: *"There's no I in team, but there are five in Individual Brilliance!"* It was a playful reminder to balance individuality with collaboration. The key is to recognise when ego might be taking over and take a moment to ask – could there be a better, more inclusive way?

In the 'busy-ness' of a kitchen, it's easy to confuse what's *urgent* with what's truly *important*. Smaller operations often skip formal training, relying on the chef's know-how or quick verbal instructions to keep things moving. But when staff call in sick, new hires arrive, or someone leaves without warning, that ad-hoc approach falls apart. That's why documenting standards isn't just helpful – it's *essential* for consistency, no matter who's on shift.

To take control, start by listing every task you handle daily or weekly. Then, apply the **Eisenhower Decision Matrix** to sort them into four buckets.

This effective tool cuts through the chaos, helping you focus on what *actually* drives your kitchen forward. Delegating the right tasks doesn't just reclaim your time – it empowers your team to step up, sharpen their skills, and own their roles. Less firefighting, more momentum.

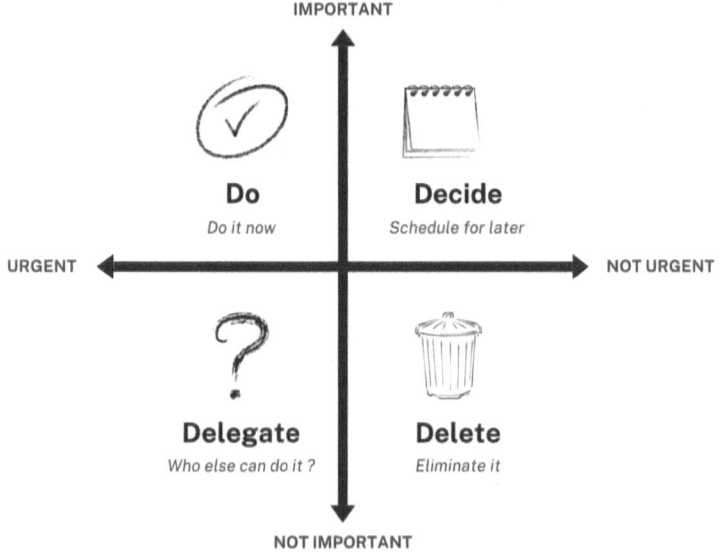

Eisenhower Decision Matrix

1. **Do.** *Urgent and Important*
   (Do these now)
2. **Decide.** *Important but Not Urgent*
   (Schedule these – this is where growth happens)
3. **Delegate.** *Urgent but Not Important*
   (Delegate these)
4. **Delete.** *Neither Urgent nor Important*
   (Ask yourself "Why am I doing this?")

Scones, Anyone?

Recently, my wife and I celebrated our wedding anniversary in the Dandenong Ranges, outside Melbourne. Among the highlights was a visit to Miss Marple's Tearoom in Sassafras, a quirky restaurant renowned for its comforting hospitality. Every time we go, they deliver a warm and welcoming experience. Over Devonshire tea, I had the chance to chat with the owner – who also happened to be serving – and I remembered her from a previous visit some years earlier. Naturally, I asked how they've maintained such a stellar legacy in hospitality.

Their secret? Simple, freshly made food and a steadfast philosophy of *"Old-Fashioned Hospitality".* They're famous for their freshly baked scones served as a loaf, toasted sandwiches and quiches. It's not fancy – just timeless, hearty food made fresh daily. Miss Marple's operates with a walk-in-only policy, is full every single day, and always has a queue of customers waiting outside. Guests are greeted with a smile at the door, orders are handwritten, and their mantra is to ensure every plate feels like a warm hug from the kitchen.

Over the past two decades, we've visited several times, and their consistency has never faltered. Attention to detail, unwavering standards and a commitment to doing the simple things well make it easy to recommend them to anyone visiting the area.

For kitchen leaders, consistency starts with solid systems and processes. But the real magic happens when your team takes ownership. At first, it might feel like you're repeating yourself

– and that's okay. Research shows it takes 5–7 repetitions for information to move from short-term to long-term memory.

So how do you help your team lock in the standards? Here are two key strategies:

1. **Involve Your Team**
   People take ownership of what they help build. Ask questions, invite feedback, and incorporate their ideas. When your team feels part of the process, they'll take greater pride in upholding the standards they've helped shape.

2. **Commit to Training**
   Training takes time and resources – but it's essential. The old school fear-based model is outdated. Today's kitchens thrive on collaboration, feedback and clear communication. Talk through customer comments, encourage team input and create a space where learning is part of the daily rhythm.

Systems are the foundation – but people are the heartbeat. Hospitality is a human-centric business so there will always be a need for ongoing training. The best operators don't treat it as an extra. They embed it into every service.

Philosophy 2.0

Having an underpinning food philosophy behind both the food and restaurant provides a guiding compass to help navigate the team, checking that everyone is on the right trajectory. In corporate terms, you might have heard of a

Vision or *Mission* statement, both of which are designed to provide a high-level guide to outcomes.

A food philosophy (also outlined in Chapter 4) resonates with chefs at a deeper level. It speaks to the emotional aspect of food, how dishes are discussed, conceived and portrayed to the customer, how they are marketed, and extends into the food you are sourcing, conversations with suppliers, producers and industry. All of the best producers I have ever met or worked with have a deep-seated passion for their produce. I'm not talking about sales reps. Their job is to sell. I'm talking about the farmer, fisherman, grower or breeder. The power of their stories and connection they have is a valued commodity, which can be harnessed and expressed through your menu and food.

Neil Perry is one of Australia's most famous chefs and was awarded an 'Icon Award' at the World's 50 Best Restaurants in 2024. Neil has defined and re-imagined Australian cuisine for over 40 years. Neil is only too happy to discuss his CARE philosophy, which he credits as a major reason for his success as a restaurateur and underpins his ethos as a chef and leader.

- *Care* for suppliers.
- *Care* for staff.
- *Care* for the community.
- *Care* for the environment.

Speaking with Neil at length around these four pillars it became evident that they are not merely a tag line, they are living and breathing factors that are woven throughout his team and restaurants. On social media, he will frequently showcase the produce he buys, singing the praises of his supply network and ensuring they are acknowledged on the menu. Back in 2006, Neil was the first Australian chef to call out David Blackmore's wagyu on his menu, trailblazing at the time yet simply true to his philosophy.

The passion and dedication he brings to hospitality is why he's so well-regarded globally for his contribution to the industry. Even today he'll still be seen working the pass at Margaret in Double Bay, hosting industry events, paying homage to his suppliers and producers and nurturing the next generation of young chefs through his systems, procedures and care for his team. That is what world-class looks like.

Key Chapter Takeaways

Consistency is king

Customers return for familiar and reliable experiences. Identify the key factors behind your success and systemise them. Creativity and innovation are vital but shouldn't disrupt the core expectations of your loyal patrons.

Address the weakest link

Your team is only as strong as its weakest link. Focus your training and support on those with the least contact time — such as casual or part-time staff. Understand their perspective, involve them in identifying challenges, and use this insight to strengthen your training and development systems.

Refine your food philosophy

Reflect on your culinary journey and articulate the principles that guide your work. What inspires you? How do you connect with your craft and communicate it to others? Use these reflections to create a high-level food philosophy that evolves with time, serving as a foundation for your leadership and menu development.

Your Mise en Place

Complete these tasks to get the most out of this chapter...

➢ **Conduct a systems audit**
List all existing systems that maintain food standards – from preparation, ordering, and plate-up to service and hygiene. Review these systems critically by asking:
- Are they effective and beneficial?
- Are they outdated and in need of revision?
- Are any redundant and ready for elimination?

➢ **Facilitate a team discussion**
Engage your team to gather their insights:
- What systems work well and add value?
- What processes feel outdated or inefficient?
- What could be improved or removed entirely?
- Encourage open feedback to refine operations collaboratively.

➢ **Prioritise training**
Focus on staff with limited hours or responsibilities. Create tailored training programs to ensure even the least-experienced team members

understand and uphold standards. By consistently revisiting and refining these principles and practices, you'll ensure your kitchen maintains its standards, grows with purpose, and builds lasting loyalty among both your team and your customers.

Chapter 12

Hone the Knife

Craft

"Cooking is about evolution not revolution."
– Heston Blumenthal

We live in the information age. Technology is rising at a rapid rate, artificial intelligence is able to instantly access, create and repurpose data and online content creation is at an all-time high. Computers provide a powerful access point to an unlimited sea of information. Algorithms curate your social media feeds to keep you engaged for prolonged periods. Anyone can pick up their smartphone, enter a handful of keywords on a specific topic or technique, and become an 'armchair expert'.

But a little bit of knowledge can be a dangerous thing, leading to overconfidence in ability and poor judgement.

Depth of knowledge takes time.

The kitchen leadership tools and techniques discussed throughout this book are given to you under the assumption that you have indeed invested the time to learn and master the basics: mise en place, methods of cookery, seasoning, flavour balance, hygiene, organisation and workflow, among others.

In this chapter, we're going to explore the importance of learning your craft in the pursuit of mastery. These kitchen leadership techniques are designed to enhance your ability to lead teams. We'll be exploring four central themes:

- Mastery
- Pedigree
- Patience
- Development

Mastery

Malcolm Gladwell's *Outliers: The Story of Success* challenges the idea of overnight success. In his book, Gladwell introduces the '10,000-Hour Rule,' suggesting that achieving mastery in any field requires roughly 10,000 hours of dedicated practice.

But it's not just about mindless repetition, like slicing onions for hours on end. It's about *deliberate* practice – pushing your limits, identifying your weaknesses, and seeking feedback

Hone the Knife

from mentors, especially those seasoned chefs who've been there and done that. Mastery isn't just about raw talent, either. It's about having the right ingredients, the right environment and the right opportunities to grow.

A young cook might spend hours practicing cooking methods, but if they're just going through the motions without focusing on technique, they're not truly improving. To grow, they need to break down each step, analyse their approach and seek guidance from a more skilled chef. It's through this deliberate, focused effort that muscle memory and instinct are built – the kind that separates a true professional from the rest.

The same applies to kitchen leadership. Developing intuition and expertise doesn't happen overnight. It requires consistent effort, a willingness to learn from both successes and failures, and the humility to seek feedback and adapt.

For me, it took 10 years on the tools in the kitchen before everything started to click into place. My mise en place was efficient, my hygiene habits were ingrained, and when presented with a task or challenge, my mind knew a dozen pathways to achieve a good result. But what really surprised me was that I was working much cleaner than ever before. My chef jacket was no longer filthy at the end of a shift. The years prior, I'd be covered head-to-toe in all kinds of food debris. After working on my craft for those 10 years, the muscle memory became second nature. Not just learning from the good habits – it was the countless fuck ups along the way that made the difference.

Secret Sauce

You win or you learn.

It's like driving a car. The first time, there's so much to take on: adjust the seat, shift the rearview mirror, put on the seatbelt, check the wipers, start the engine, indicate, check over your shoulder, and slowly accelerate out from the curb. There's a lot of thinking and coordination going into just getting that car moving. As you become more proficient, these tasks are done automatically through muscle memory. Suddenly, you might find yourself 30 kilometres down the road, listening to your playlist and wondering how you got there so fast.

I implore you to embrace this time mastering the basics. Don't rush it. Adopting an 'apprentice mindset' allows you to absorb information without the additional pressure of leadership expectation. Prior to taking on additional responsibility, soak up the knowledge on offer from the sources around you – the team you are working with, supplier events, reading, dining out and connecting with industry leaders through social media.

Work smarter, not harder.

Pedigree
Leadership skills, like cooking, are consciously learned and subconsciously assimilated while working with great people – the good habits and the bad habits. Many of the world's top chefs have a pedigree of training they attribute to their success. Gordon Ramsay often credits his time working with Marco Pierre White as a pivotal point in his career. Cooking is a learned skill – and it's your choice to

determine what lessons you require at each stage in your career, then pursue them.

Seeking out learning and development opportunities will fast track your kitchen leadership. Immersive activities such as attending cooking classes with experts from alternative cuisines, participating in competitions, industry organisations and seeking out mentors all have a role to play. The skills to be gained from reading is not to be underestimated. Cookbooks are an intimate conversation with the author, full of their ideas, wisdom and knowledge. It takes a massive investment of time for the author to bring them to life, and we (as readers) have the chance to absorb their knowledge for a small dollar investment.

When I arrived in the UK as a chef de partie, I secured a job at Harvey's restaurant under French chef Daniel Galmiche. The team were driven, the kitchen culture felt right, and the food was immaculate. I recall Daniel saying to me on my first shift, "Just take whatever you think you know and park it at the door. I will show you the way we do things here." He was respectful of my past training but also appreciative that I had a lot to learn. Working for two years at a Michelin-starred restaurant under Chef Daniel was a highlight in my culinary journey. I didn't realise at the time, but the depth of experience I gained was shaping my mindset and my career. And it wasn't just his knowledge I was absorbing; it was from those people he had worked with and the entire 'pedigree'.

Who are you currently working with? Have you taken the time to ask about their background, training, triumphs and failures? How are you shaping your culinary family tree so that it fits into where you would like you career to go? What habits will you take forward as a kitchen leader, and which ones are holding you back?

Patience
Over the years, I've come to deeply appreciate the art of gardening. There's something really satisfying about watching seedlings transform into thriving plants and eventually be ready to harvest. This connection to nature and the cycle of growth is a constant reminder of patience and timing – qualities that extend beyond the soil. My understanding of the importance of cultivating patience deepened when I took a team of apprentices to assist building a school garden in the early days of Stephanie Alexander's Kitchen Garden Foundation.

Founded by the passionate chef and produce advocate, the foundation has been transforming the way children experience food since 2001. Piloted at Melbourne's Collingwood College, the pioneering garden program introduces primary school children to the joys of growing, harvesting, and cooking their own fresh produce. The program shows that nurturing plants is about more than sustenance – it's a hands-on lesson in patience, responsibility and the rewards of effort over time.

There's a saying attributed to the Chinese philosopher Lao Tzu: *"Nature does not hurry, yet everything is accomplished"*. To me, it's a reminder that patience and steady progress often lead to the best outcomes.

Hone the Knife

A common mistake many chefs make is rushing for promotions too quickly. I believe this sets you up for failure. Instead, take your time to experiment, fail, learn and grow before stepping into leadership roles. Embrace this phase – it's invaluable. Don't waste it.

Gardening has taught me that experience can't be forced. The only way to gain it is by living through it, one season at a time.

Honing Your Knife

One of my first roles after qualifying as a chef was working in a five-star hotel. Like a lot of large hotels of the era it was a wonderful ecosystem of international talent – the sous chef was German, the head chef was Australian and the executive pastry chef was Irish. We had a brigade of around 80 chefs servicing the banquets, the fine dining restaurant, café, room service, buffet and an amazing Japanese restaurant.

I had never worked in such a large brigade, and the learning opportunities were everywhere. Mind you, there was the standard political undertone synonymous with five-star hotels at that time, and a very competitive hierarchy among the commis and demi chefs, all vying to get promoted and climb the kitchen 'ladder'.

The Japanese fine dining restaurant absolutely fascinated me. Every time there was an order for sashimi, seafood or lobster, I would have the opportunity to visit the Japanese kitchen to seek the required ingredients. I wanted to work there to learn from the brigade but I was quickly advised it was for Japanese chefs only. They had a particular discipline and skill set that I had yet to acquire. However, this did not deter me from finding any opportunity to be in that kitchen, watching and learning.

One of the things that stuck with me through all these years is that about one hour before every shift the chefs would be in the kitchen sharpening and honing their knives. It was kind of a daily ritual for the brigade....the sound of the knife blades being rhythmically honed across the wet stone again and again was hypnotic. It seemed to set the tempo for the mise en place and service to follow. Such was the dedication to their craft and dedication to their tools.

As an emerging kitchen leader, you need to constantly hone your most powerful tool – your mind. Reading, discussing, seeking knowledge to evolve your skills, bringing new ideas to challenge old problems. Whether it be refining your communication skills, running effective meetings, practicing active listening or giving constructive feedback, evolution is key.

Keep your team's culinary knowledge expanding by asking team members to cook the staff meal, create specials, refine techniques and invite suppliers to showcase new ingredients or discuss culinary trends.

But the most critical factor for you is the inner work of developing your self-awareness. Identifying areas for improvement, letting go of personal biases and being aware of your weaknesses. There's a famous proverb by Abraham Lincoln, "Give me six hours to chop down a tree, and I'll spend the first four sharpening the axe".

Follow the White Rabbit

If you've made it this far – well done! Your appetite for knowledge and development is to be commended. You might be feeling a bit like Neo in the Matrix once he has downloaded Kung Fu. Kitchen leadership 'mastery' isn't about brute force or just putting in the hours. It's about a profound shift in awareness. I hope this book was able to complement your existing skills, highlight areas for improvement and provide practical examples you can relate to across the four masteries of Kitchen Leadership: People, Finance, Safety and Quality.

Many of the concepts covered might seem abstract at first, as you already have an abundance of existing habits in place that have gotten you to this level. Now you've been challenged to see the kitchen in a new light.

With consistent practice and a dedicated mindset, these concepts will start to click. You'll begin to see the connections, anticipate the needs of your team, and act with the confidence that comes through experience. And remember, when the student is ready, the teacher will appear.

It will not always be easy, but the best lessons are the hardest ones.

Key Chapter Takeaways

Depth of knowledge

True mastery in any craft, especially cooking, requires years of practice and learning. While modern technology provides easy access to information, it can't replace the time and hands-on experience necessary to develop deep expertise.

Mastery

The journey to mastery is about transcending limitations and making extraordinary skills feel like second nature. It requires dedication over time – around 10,000 hours or roughly 8-10 years – before muscle memory, efficiency and intuition take over in the kitchen.

Pedigree

Leadership skills, like cooking, are learned both consciously and subconsciously. By working with great mentors, you absorb both their good and bad habits, which influences your own leadership style.

Patience

You can't rush experience or success – both are cultivated over time through trial, error, and growth.

Hone the Knife

> The process of learning, failing, and trying again is invaluable in shaping your skills and leadership approach.

Your Mise en Place

Complete these tasks to get the most out of this chapter...

➤ **10,000 hours**
Reflect on the knowledge you've gained during your 10,000 hours in the kitchen. How has this shaped you as a leader? Consider the skills, methods, and processes that have become second nature to you. Where does your mastery lie?

➤ **Review your habits**
Think about the mentors and leaders you've worked with throughout your career. What lessons have they imparted? What positive habits will you adopt, and what negative ones will you avoid? Leverage these experiences to guide your leadership journey.

➤ **Hone your knives**
Mastery requires constant refinement. Your tools of trade, whether physical or mental, must be cared for and sharpened regularly. What will you commit to in terms of development over the next 12 months?

Afterword

The Final Course

I know way too many chefs who have burned out. Fuck, I've been there too...on several occasions. Constant pressure. Staff issues. Equipment breaking down. The pursuit of perfection. Overworked. Underpaid. Frenetic pace. Too much prep. Apprentice needs stitches. Kitchenhand got deported. Being over-responsible. Exhausted from driving the team. Frustrated by the skill of the wait staff. Dealing with painful customers. Negotiating with suppliers. Wading through political bullshit. Being harassed by administration managers who just don't seem to understand. Planning the next function. Processing paperwork. Replying to emails. Riding the adrenalin of service. Losing my shit. Hitting targets. Chasing accolades. Dropping the next social media post. Hitting deadlines. Wearing too many hats – manager, coach, mentor, confidant, psychologist, teacher, friend.

And that's just Monday!

Secret Sauce

It only takes one small idea to alter your career trajectory and I hope you found some solace in these pages. To close out this banquet of kitchen leadership ideas, my last offering is this:

When it all seems too much, when you're exhausted, hating on the customers, the game, the industry. Before you throw in the towel or crumble on the kitchen floor, just take four seconds to breathe and remember the feeling you had the first time you cooked a meal and received a "thank you".

The simplicity of that moment.

The smile you had, the warm feeling inside, the self-belief, the calling to your craft.

In that moment, it was all about simple act of expressing your creativity and practicing your craft. The purest act of alchemy.

That's what cooking is all about.

Engaging all of your senses and creating a meal to bring happiness and nourishment.

Try not to over-complicate things and get back to basics.......
Chef!

About the Author

Kitchen leadership is a niche Glenn has come to define through years of experience, shifting from running busy kitchens to mentoring, training, building teams and leading food strategy.

Simply stated – Glenn solves leadership and team performance issues in the food industry.

While the principles of leadership are universal, Glenn has the unique ability to speak the language of hospitality on multiple levels. His path hasn't been without challenges – he's been frustrated, exhausted and screwed over. He's been burned….and been burned out.

Glenn's journey began with a traditional four-year chef's apprenticeship, during which he earned the title of *Apprentice of the Year*. With a deep hunger for knowledge, he embarked on a career that spanned five-star hotels, fine dining establishments, Canadian ski fields, Michelin-starred kitchens in the UK and more. Each step refined his craft and expanded his perspective.

Secret Sauce

The turning point came during his time as Training and Development Chef at Fifteen Melbourne, working alongside Tobie Puttock. Inspired by Jamie Oliver's Fifteen Foundation in London, the Melbourne program aimed to provide disadvantaged youth with training and a pathway into the hospitality industry.

While Glenn's passion for food had always been strong, this role shifted his focus toward people – mentoring, training and supporting young chefs as they navigated the challenges of the industry and developed life skills. Fuelled by a drive to make a meaningful impact, he poured himself into the role with relentless intensity.

The accompanying TV documentary, Jamie's Kitchen Australia, brought significant attention to the program. On one hand, it ensured the restaurant was fully booked, creating countless opportunities for the apprentices. On the other hand, it pushed the young team – and Glenn – to the brink, with long hours and relentless pressure. At the same time, Glenn and his wife, Niki, welcomed their first son, adding to an already intense period.

Despite the inspiration he drew from the program's transformative impact, Glenn found himself unequipped for the weight of the emotional load. Burnout became a reality. It was a wake-up call, prompting Glenn to adjust his career trajectory, seeking out the coaching knowledge to complement his leadership skills. He completed an Advanced Diploma in Hospitality Management, Certificate in Training and Assessment, and is a Master Practitioner in

About the Author

Neuro-Linguistic Programming. Glenn is also an NLP Certified Meta-Coach and holds a Diploma of Positive Psychology and Wellbeing.

He went on to launch a cooking school and demonstration kitchen, designed corporate team-building programs, hosted a podcast, was food producer for MasterChef Australia, and held leadership roles including Executive Chef, Food Development Manager and National Culinary Manager. With nearly three decades in the industry, the past ten years have been dedicated to mastering and teaching leadership.

Empowering people has become Glenn's passion, with food as the common thread.

Glenn has seen talented individuals burn out, overwhelmed by leadership roles without proper management training. Secret Sauce is the guide he wishes he had when transitioning through the various stages of his career.

Just like cooking, leadership is a skill to be learned and practiced. Through this guide, Glenn aims to share the proven recipe for success – helping kitchen leaders empower their teams, drive high performance and grow as leaders themselves.

His advice is clear: start by applying these principles to yourself. Because all true leadership begins with the same essential ingredient: **You**.

The Next Steps

How to Stay in Touch with Me

If this book has whet your appetite for Kitchen Leadership then here are some bonus offers for you:

1. Mindfood E-Newsletter
Sign up to my newsletter to receive leadership hacks, musings and thought-provoking ideas each month. It's easy to digest and loaded with tips to fuel your personal development. Scan the QR code or sign up at www.glennflood.com.

2. Exclusive Access to the Kitchen Leadership Self Audit

This self-audit is designed to help you reflect on your current leadership performance, giving you a clear picture of where you're excelling and where there's room to grow. To get started, scan the QR code and use the code **"Self-Audit"** in the message box. Your free Kitchen Leadership Self-Audit will be sent to you. It's self-paced and will assess your strengths, identify opportunities for improvement and set you on a development pathway.

3. Book a Complimentary 1:1 Mentor Session

Ready to level up your kitchen leadership? In just 20 minutes, Glenn will help you cut through the noise with tailored advice on communication, team performance or professional development. Come away with clear, practical steps you can apply immediately. Scan the QR code to book, and enter "Secret Sauce" to unlock this special offer. It's your first step toward leading with confidence and impact.

4. Kitchen Therapy Podcast

Hosted by Glenn and Tobie, tune into casual and insightful conversations with some of the best chefs in the business. Available on Spotify and Apple Podcasts.

5. Connecting on Social

Connect with me on LinkedIn, Facebook or Instagram **@glenn_flood**

Learn more at www.glennflood.com

Keynote Speaker

Photo by Kerry Herschell

With 25+ years in professional kitchens, food media, and hospitality leadership, Glenn Flood brings grounded insight, real-world experience, and lasting impact to every stage.

His keynotes blend compelling stories, practical tools, and a relatable, down-to-earth style – ideal for industries where pressure is high, and leadership matters most.

Popular Keynote Topics:

1. The Secret Sauce for High-Performing Teams
From Michelin-starred kitchens to executive boardrooms, Glenn shares the essential ingredients for trust, collaboration, and results – even in the heat of service.

2. Navigating Leadership Transitions
One of the most challenging transitions in any industry is moving from a technical role into leadership. Based on the book Secret Sauce, this keynote supports those moving from the tools into managing teams. Learn to lead with clarity, inspire others and avoid burnout in a rapidly transforming world.

3. Resilience and Mental Wellbeing

In high-pressure environments like hospitality, resilience isn't a nice-to-have — it's essential. Drawing on his work with Jamie Oliver's Fifteen Foundation, along with studies in neuroscience and developmental coaching, Glenn shares real-world strategies to enhance mindset, create a supportive team culture and sustain performance.

Why Choose Glenn?

Proven Track Record: Glenn has worked with top brands like MasterChef, Dan Murphys, Fonterra, Coles and Foodservice Australia delivering impactful keynotes, masterclasses and training programs.

Authentic Storytelling: With decades of hands-on experience, Glenn's presentations are filled with real-life leadership examples and actionable takeaways.

Tailored Content: Glenn customises his keynotes to meet your audience where they are, ensuring maximum relevance and impact.

Glenn delivers more than a keynote – he delivers perspective, purpose, and practical change.

Ready to inspire your team?

Get directly in touch via email at **glenn@glennflood.com.**

Bibliography

Shewry, Ben. *Uses for Obsession: A (Chef's) Memoir*. Murdoch Books, 2024.

Robinson, Richard NS, et al. *The Mental Health and Wellbeing of Chefs in Commercial Kitchens: An Australasian Study*. Tuwhera, Auckland University of Technology, 2023.

Cerasa, Antonio, et al. *"Work-Related Stress Among Chefs: A Predictive Model of Health Complaints."* Frontiers in Public Health, vol. 8, 2020, p. 68. *Frontiers*, doi:10.3389/fpubh.2020.00068.

Clear, James. *Atomic Habits: Tiny Changes, Remarkable Results – An Easy & Proven Way to Build Good Habits & Break Bad Ones*. Avery, 2018.

Bregman, Peter. *Four Seconds: All the Time You Need to Replace Counter-Productive Habits with Ones That Really Work*. HarperOne, 2015.

Csikszentmihalyi, Mihaly. *Flow: The Psychology of Optimal Experience*. Harper & Row, 1990.

Seligman, Martin E. P. *Flourish: A Visionary New Understanding of Happiness and Well-being*. Free Press, 2011.

Duckworth, Angela. *Grit: The Power of Passion and Perseverance*. Scribner, 2016.

Shewry, Ben. Origin: *The Food of Ben Shewry*. Phaidon Press, 2018.

Koch, Richard. *The 80/20 Principle, Expanded and Updated: The Secret to Achieving More with Less*. Paperback ed., Currency, 1999.

Guidara, Will. *Unreasonable Hospitality: The Power of Giving People More Than They Expect*. Optimism Press, 2022.

Charnas, Dan. *Work Clean: The Life-Changing Power of Mise-En-Place to Organize Your Life, Work, and Mind*. Rodale Books, 2016.

Rubin, Rick. *The Creative Act: A Way of Being*. Penguin Press, 2023.

Trotter, Charlie. *Charlie Trotter's Chicago*. Ten Speed Press, 1994.

Gladwell, Malcolm. *Outliers: The Story of Success*. Little, Brown and Company, 2008.

Notes

www.ingramcontent.com/pod-product-compliance
Lightning Source LLC
Chambersburg PA
CBHW030316080526
44584CB00012B/590